LANDSCAPE CONSTRUCTION
VOLUME 1

LANDSCAPE CONSTRUCTION
VOLUME 1

WALLS, FENCES AND RAILINGS

C. A. Fortlage
E. T. Phillips

Gower

Published by
Gower Publishing Company Limited
Gower House
Croft Road
Aldershot
Hants GU11 3HR
England

Gower Publishing Company
Old Post Road
Brookfield
Vermont 05036
USA

British Library Cataloguing in Publication Data
Fortlage, Catharine
    Landscape construction. Vol. 1:
    Walls, fences and railings.
    I. Title II. Phillips, Elizabeth
    712

ISBN 0 566 09041 4

Reprinted 2000

Printed in Great Britain by
Antony Rowe Ltd, Chippenham, Wiltshire

CONTENTS

TABLES

FIGURES

Plates

FOREWORD

Landscape is becoming of increasing importance to both urban and rural developments, but sadly many good landscape designs are marred by the unfortunate detailing of the hard landscape. When completed this series will provide the first comprehensive work on construction written specifically for the landscape designer, who, until now has had to rely on extracts from technical information, manufacturers' catalogues, British Standards, and architectural textbooks for information.

The three volumes of Landscape Construction will cover all aspects of hard landscape building and constructon work. Basic buildings construction is an essential part of the training and professional skills of the landscape designer, and these texts will fulfil the need for straightforward and clearly illustrated information on each subject. There are plentiful illustrations supplemented by photographs on all aspects of hard landscape.

This first volume covers the principles of construction of brick and stone landscape walls, fences, security barriers, gates, and railings, together with their fittings and finishes. The other two volumes will cover paving and road surfaces, drainage, services, light structures, earth and water retaining structures, and will include a section on construction failures and remedial work.

Together the three volumes of Landscape Construction will be an essential desk-top reference work for the landscape designer who is concerned with good standards of construction and workmanship; and should do much to give the student of landscape design a sound technical foundation for his professional work.

Professor Derk Lovejoy
MA(Harvard) DipTP FRIBA FRTPI PPILA FRSA FIHT

INTRODUCTION TO VOLUME 1

This volume deals with elements of landscape construction which are required to provide enclosure, privacy, demarcation of land, shelter and security. These include freestanding brick and stone walls, fences, gates and railings and their construction or erection with their fixings and fittings.

It is divided into ten sections: walls generally; brick walls; freestanding landscape walls; site supervision of brickwork; natural and man-made stone walling; fences; gates; railings; preservative treatment and painting; and site supervision of fencing work. Each section describes the materials, construction and constraints relevant to the subject, with figures and photographs to illustrate important points.

1 WALLS

The most conspicuous item in the landscape design is usually the landscape walls. This term is used to distinguish ornamental and screening walls from those which carry structural loads other than their own weight. The design of such walls is the province of the structural engineer or the architect, and it is inadvisable for landscape designers to undertake the design of these walls unless they have had the necessary training in structural design. It is more efficient to employ a structural engineer to design load-bearing structures than to attempt to design them without the necessary training, especially as there is little published information dedicated to the construction of land-scape walls. *The Design of Freestanding Walls*, published by the Brick Development Association is not in line with current British Standards on wall and foundation design.

The first step is to establish the client's brief concerning the size, location and construction of all landscape walls on the site, and although each project will have different requirements the following points are typical of many contracts:

- *Security* The most critical factor is security. Are the walls intended to keep the public in or out? Are intruders a mild nuisance or a serious threat to the property? Perhaps a brick wall 1.8 m high will be sufficient to keep people out, or it may be necessary to provide a smooth unclimbable wall 3.5 m high. The cost of very secure walling is substantial so it is important to get the budget allocation for security correct at the outset. If the landscape designer does not consider security seriously he may leave the client vulnerable to expensive depredations, caused by theft or vandalism.
- *Function* The work which the wall is called on to perform must be stated. The effect on the wall of vandals, active adults, animals, vehicles or children will dictate the type and construction of the wall. A wall which has to direct amiable visitors to the most charming view, with intermittent glimpses of an attractive landscape, will be completely differ-

1

ent from one which has to screen car-parking areas, or one which has to give privacy and protection to residents in a crime-prone area.

- *Legal constraints* Any legal restraints on the height or type of wall must be ascertained. Planning permission may be needed for boundary walls in conservation areas and other protected areas, and the local planning authority may impose conditions on materials and finishes as part of the landscape design control which is usually dealt with in the 'reserved matters' part of planning permission. This point is particularly important in the stone building areas of Britain, where natural or man-made stone may be specified by the local authority. The highway authorities may impose height limitations on walls where they border a highway, especially where sight lines at junctions are involved. In some private estates there are controls on the type and height of walls which may be erected even in private gardens and there may also be covenants on the land which affect the materials used for walls. Local authorities usually have standard specifications for projects such as schools, housing estates, and parks which must be followed.
- *Emergency access* The section on Gates deals with access by emergency vehicles but the landscape designer should remember to discuss the type and position of gates with the fire brigade, the police and the ambulance service at an early stage in the project.
- *Maintenance costs* The cost of maintenance operations may be an important consideration to the client and his maintenance budget should be considered before the walls are designed, since regular cleaning of graffitti or repairing damage by vehicles may be necessary.

The main material used for the construction of walls is brick, especially in the south and centre of England and, nowadays, even in traditional stone building districts since the cost of winning and working stone is considerably greater than that of making brick. Natural stone blocks cannot be mass produced to the same extent as bricks, and the cost of transport from distant quarries is a significant part of the cost, except for drystone dykeing where the material lies close to hand. The rural field boundaries called drystone walls or dykes are a regional specialty where the material is naturally occurring stone found in outcrops or collected from the surface; such walls are not normally detailed by the landscape designer, but are contracted out to a specialist wall builder, often trained by one of the government agencies engaged in promoting rural crafts. This volume deals with brickwork and stonework and includes fine work carried out by highly skilled craftsmen as well as with the more utilitarian walls associated with housing estates and supermarkets. Because of the comparative difficulty and cost of constructing natural stone walls more emphasis has been given to the design and construction of brick walls rather than to stone walls.

The landscape designer will find that the word 'masonry' is used today to describe brick and concrete block construction as well as stonework; this is a denigration of the superior knowledge and skill of the stonemason, who was traditionally the senior master craftsman on any building job. However good the bricklayer may be, he does not possess that ability to understand, handle and carve natural close grained stone (known as freestone) which is the special skill of the mason.

It should be the duty of the landscape designer to press for good workmanship in all construction, and good craftsmanship in skilled work such as arches and ornamental brickwork, whenever and wherever possible (though no purpose is served by pushing the client over his budget to the extinction of the project). A thorough knowledge of all aspects of brick- and stonework is essential if the landscape designer is to be able to select the appropriate style and quality of materials; to design stable, efficient structures capable of fulfilling their intended function; and to ensure that the work is carried out correctly in accordance with established good practice and in compliance with the contract documents. Although the contractor is directly responsible for safety on site, the landscape designer has a moral responsibility in addition to his statutory 'duty of care' to ensure that all safety precautions are followed.

2 BRICK LANDSCAPE WALLS

This description covers freestanding walls up to three metres high which do not perform any structural function and which do not form part of a building. The following sections deal with the construction of the walls and their foundations, reinforced brickwork, brick bonding, copings, damp-proof courses, mortars, and the construction of openings, arches and ornamental brickwork, as well as advice to the landscape designer on site workmanship. As more and more architects are including fine craftsmanship in brick and stone in their buildings, the landscape designer will be expected to follow their lead in creating interesting, elegant and soundly built landscape walls.

2.1 TERMS USED IN BRICKWORK

A full glossary of the building terms used in this volume is included at the end of the text, but it is convenient to describe the main terms for brickwork at the beginning of the construction sections.

A 'course' is one horizontal layer of bricks plus one mortar joint.

The 'bond' is the chosen arrangement of bricks in the wall, designed to give strength, stability, cohesion, and a good appearance to the wall. Strength and appearance are dictated by the bond of the brickwork, so that the selection of the bond is a matter of great importance.

A 'pier' is strictly speaking, a freestanding column of brickwork, usually supporting a beam. An 'attached pier' is the term used for the extra thickness of brickwork at the end or middle of a long freestanding wall which stabilizes the structure and is often used to strengthen the wall where it carries a gate.

'Copings' are the capping laid on a wall to throw rain off the brickwork and to provide a hard frost- and damage-resistant finish.

Plate 1   Traditional brick landscape wall   *A one brick thick wall with one and a half brick thick piers and plinth. The wall is corbelled out at the top and has a tiled capping finished with a ridge tile. The pier caps are built up from tiles corbelled out, and the ball on top is made from shaped bricks. A wall like this is unlikely to be designed today, but it shows how a rich effect can be created using only two materials: brick and tile.*

The 'damp proof course' or DPC is a layer of impervious bricks, slates or other waterproof material laid between two courses of bricks 150 mm above ground level to prevent damp creeping up the wall. There is also a DPC of non-slip bituminous material under the coping if waterproof copings are not used.

'Fair-face' means that the face of the wall is carefully laid with all the bricks in the same plane, and usually requires the joints to be pointed after laying. A wall that is specified to be 'fair-faced both sides' must be at least 215 mm thick, as a half-brick wall cannot be laid fair-face due to the variation in the shapes and sizes of bricks.

The 'brickie' is the bricklayer ('sparks' is the electrician, 'chippie' is the carpenter).

2.2   FACTORS AFFECTING THE CHOICE OF BRICKS

The selection of the most satisfactory brick for the landscape walls is not just a matter of choosing the colour and texture which is appropriate to the character of the design, but of specifying a brick which will perform satisfactorily under all foreseeable conditions of use. It is worthwhile listing the factors which are most likely to be met, which include the following:

Natural factors

- Chemical soil conditions which will attack bricks in contact with the ground (especially in the case of retaining walls).
- Acid rain from local or remote industries.
- Salt spray from marine climate or winter salting on adjacent roads.
- Wind erosion from wind-borne sand or grit particles, which may occur close to industrial sites or in sand-dune areas.
- Continual wetting and drying cycles which dissolve the free salts in the bricks, producing harmless but unsightly white efflorescence all over the face of a brick wall.
- Frost action on underburnt or unsuitable bricks, causing spalling of the brick face or frost action on both bricks and mortar.
- Continuously damp conditions which permit algal growth.
- Water run-off which may contain iron or other salts, and may cause irremovable staining, eg copper flashing, metal fixings.

Man-made factors

- Vandalism, which may include scarring the face with steel tools, surface scratching, various graffiti made with paints, dyes, felt pens, creosote, and so on.
- Staining from industrial processes, paints, oils, and many other special chemicals, which will need special precautions. Walls in industrial estates and science parks suffer from the propensity of the owners to pile old chemical drums, empty paint tins and similar rubbish against the nearest wall. Even sand, grass clippings, or compost can stain brick walls irremedially. The use of engineering brick is recommended for these situations if the extra cost can be justified.
- Car exhausts are often a source of unsightly stains on dwarf boundary walls.
- Scraping and scarring from vehicles, shopping trolleys, bicycles, forklift trucks, and so forth.
- Unskilled cleaning with acids or other unsuitable methods. This is a

source of despair to historic building guardians, and can cause severe damage to fine brickwork.

2.3 TYPES OF BRICK SUITABLE FOR LANDSCAPE WORK

Some brickmakers claim that the architect today has a choice of over a thousand different coloured and textured bricks, though not all of these are useful to the landscape designer since many are only suitable for internal construction. Bricks are generally divided by the construction industry into three main groups: commons, facings, and engineering bricks, which are all discussed below. There are, of course, many other types of special brick, such as refractory bricks for chimney work, but these are unlikely to interest the landscape designer. There are three main materials used for the manufacture of bricks: treated natural clay, calcium silicate (flint-lime bricks or sand-lime bricks), and concrete. The majority of bricks used in landscape work are clay bricks, since these offer the most attractive range of colours and textures, but calcium silicate bricks are satisfactory as far as structural strength and durability are concerned and may be used equally well. Concrete bricks with similar properties are available, and most 'stone' walling blocks used for residential boundary walls are technically concrete bricks with more or less decorative finishes. Because bricks are a structural material of major importance, they are controlled by a number of British Standards, though as these are mainly concerned with establishing the structural strength and durability of bricks for building work, the landscape designer may find that bricks which do not meet the rigorous standards required by the BSs may be quite adequate for low landscape walls. The quality of clay bricks is controlled by BS 3921:1985, that of calcium silicate bricks by BS 187:1978, and concrete bricks for structural work are controlled by BS 6073: Part 1:1971. (See Figure 2.1)

Clay bricks

Commons are the cheapest material, and are rather plain bricks of uninteresting appearance, mainly used for work below ground, under rendering, and where cost limits take priority over all other considerations, although some commons are pleasing enough to be used for walls where appearance is not the main design consideration. Facings are a more decorative brick with an attractive appearance used for visible parts of walls. Engineering bricks are dense, strong bricks intended to support heavy loads or to provide water barriers. Except for engineering bricks, which have to meet very strict structural standards, bricks covered by BS 3921 must have a minimum crushing strength of 5.2 N/mm^2.

With regard to weather resistance – which is a matter of importance to landscape designers – BS 3921 classifies bricks as shown in Table 2.1.

Table 2.1
Durability of bricks

FL   Frost resistant with low salt content
FN   Frost resistant with normal salt content
ML   Moderately frost resistant with low salt content
MN   Moderately frost resistant with normal salt content
OL   Not frost resistant with low salt content
ON   Not frost resistant with normal salt content

Table 2.2
Choice of bricks for given locations

Position	Brick type
brickwork at ground level well-drained ground	FL FN ML MN
brickwork at ground level badly drained ground	FL FN
brickwork below ground	FL FN ML MN
damp-proof courses	FL FN ML MN engineering
copings to walls	FL FN ML MN engineering
brick-on-edge copings	FL FN engineering
earth retaining walls with waterproofed retaining face	FL FN ML MN engineering
manholes, silt pits	FL FN engineering

The damage caused by frost is due to the expansion of the water in the brick when it becomes ice; this expansion can be as much as 9 per cent of the volume of the water. Severity of frost is not the main cause of damage; it is the recurrence of alternate freezing and thawing which does most harm, including spalling, flaking and deterioration of the mortar joints. FL and FN quality bricks are very frost and weather resistant; ML and MN quality bricks are durable but not capable of standing up to extreme weather conditions; and OL and ON are intended more for internal work and are not weather resistant (they are mostly used for partitions and other indoor brickwork). The salt content of the bricks gives some guide to the amount of efflorescence to be expected, and while this whitish encrustation does no physical harm to the wall it will do no good at all to the landscape designer's reputation with his client. The selection of bricks for frost resistance, durability and water resistance must take priority over their selection for appearance. The Table 2.2 gives a general guide to the selection of bricks for a range of situations. Descriptions of the types of mortar appropriate to these situations are given in the later section on mortars.

Commons

Commons are made from rather dull clay, and are usually wirecut, that is, the prepared clay is extruded from a die and cut off into brick lengths by a cutting wire. They are perfectly suitable for all normal purposes, but because they are not attractive, their use in good quality work is confined to brickwork out of sight, such as parts of walls below ground or where the face will be rendered. They are also used as backing in one- or two-brick-thick walls where the appearance of the reverse side is not so important and it is needlessly expensive to use facing bricks throughout. They may be the only type of brick available within the cost limits of low-cost housing contracts. Perforated bricks are an alternative to frogs in order to ensure mechanical bonding of the mortar. They also save weight and allow reinforcing rods to be inserted for the full height of the wall in order to increase its strength without increasing the thickness.

Commons are sometimes finished during manufacture to create a more interesting surface; this may be on one header and one stretcher face only. These finishes include dragging to form irregular or wavy lines, facing the brick with coloured sand (this is easily removed if the wall is subjected to abrasion), or controlled burning in the kiln which produces light and dark patches. These textured bricks can then be used as inferior facings, though they are never as attractive or as pleasantly textured as natural clay surfaces.

Facings

Facings include an enormously wide range of bricks with colours varying from almost white to the deepest dark red and from pale yellow to dark brown, and surface textures ranging from hard smooth surfaces like pottery to very rough-textured rural facings. They can be wirecut, machine, or hand-moulded. The cheapest facings are wirecut, which leaves a slightly 'dragged' face. Although these are perfectly satisfactory as regards strength and durability, they will give a more monotonous appearance to the wall than the rich texture created by moulded bricks.

Next in quality are the pressed bricks which are made by pressing the clay mechanically into individual moulds and these bricks have a 'frog' or sinking formed in the mould on one side which distinguishes them from wirecuts. The frog saves some clay without any sacrifice of strength and provides a good key for the mortar joints; bricks with frogs are easier for the brickie to handle. For at least two generations, architects and bricklayers have argued about the position of the frog, whether the bricks should be laid frog up or frog down. While there are innumerable reasons for choosing either position the landscape designer need not be too concerned about this argument, since if there were a real advantage in one method or the other it would have been established by now.

Handmade facings are the most expensive, since each measured lump of clay is pressed into an individual mould by a craftsman brickmaker. After firing it has a slightly different shape or shade of colour, and the resulting brickwork has a very definite character which can produce a wall of great charm and liveliness. Because of the high cost of manufacture, only the best clays are used for handmade bricks.

There is a very wide range of weight, water absorption and compressive strength in facings; for example, Butterley's Milton Hall Mild Stock brick is a natural-textured brick with a compressive strength of 12.0 N/mm^2, water absorption 27 per cent, and weighs 159 kg/m^2 of half-brick wall when built, whereas the Waingroves Kedleston Red is a smooth-surfaced hard-arrised brick, with a compressive strength of 75.0 N/mm^2, absorption 6 per cent, weight 183 kg/m^2. Obviously, these two types of brick are suitable for two quite different situations. The harder, more water-resistant brick is suitable for situations exposed to driving rain, and the softer brick for a more sheltered site where a gentler appearance is desirable.

In addition to the choice of clays, surface texture, and colour, it is sometimes possible to obtain a wider choice by selecting bricks burnt in different ways. Most bricks are fired in continuous kilns which pass the bricks through a carefully regulated burning process, thus producing a fairly standardized brick with little wastage. Some variation occurs because bricks on the outside of the kiln pack, and bricks which are wetter or dryer than others, will burn slightly differently. There may also be small variations in kiln temperature, and these will also produce different coloured and sized bricks. However, in order to sell bricks which comply with the British Standards and with the brickmaker's own standards of colour and texture consistency, many of these bricks will be rejected at the brickworks.

A few small brickworks still have individual kilns where each charge is fired separately, producing bricks which are much more variable, and thus giving an attractive range of colour and texture in each firing. The landscape designer must check these small-kiln bricks to ensure that he is not getting bricks which are either underburnt, when they will crumble under weather stress, or overburnt, when they will be deformed and may shatter under structural stress. It used to be normal practice for the designer to choose bricks at the brickworks and even to specify the degree of burning required, but this is no longer practicable for the majority of contracts.

For important work it is necessary to ask the brick supplier to say where the proposed bricks can be seen, and preferably where they have been built and weathered for some years. Even with carefully controlled brickmaking, bricks being a natural material will vary from batch to batch. For this reason, *all* the bricks for a job must be ordered from the same batch, and the bricklayer must be instructed by the contractor to mix all pallet loads evenly throughout the work if a good appearance is to be achieved. For very important and prestigious contracts the architect may order special bricks to be made to his specification provided that the requirement is sufficient to justify the special run. The landscape designer who is working on one of these

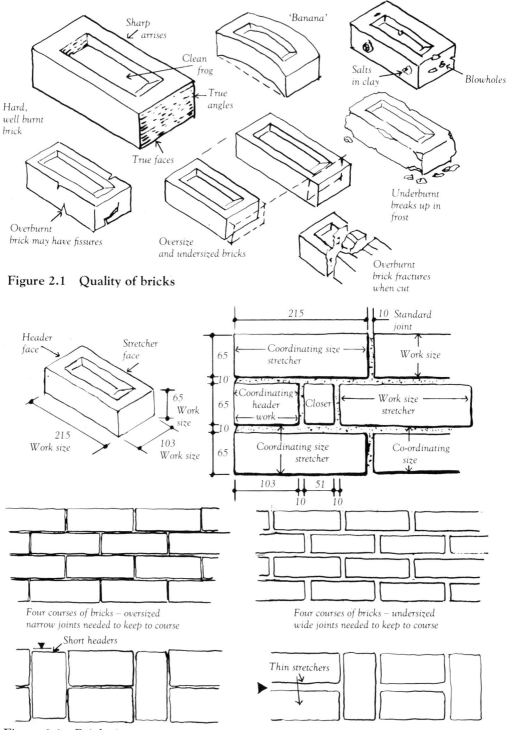

Figure 2.1   Quality of bricks

Sharp arrises

Clean frog

'Banana'

Salts in clay

Blowholes

True angles

Hard, well burnt brick

True faces

Underburnt breaks up in frost

Overburnt brick may have fissures

Oversize and undersized bricks

Overburnt brick fractures when cut

Header face

Stretcher face

215 Standard joint

Coordinating size stretcher

Work size

65 Work size

10

Coordinating header work

Closer

Work size stretcher

215 Work size

103 Work size

Coordinating size stretcher

Co-ordinating size

103   51

10   10

Four courses of bricks – oversized narrow joints needed to keep to course

Four courses of bricks – undersized wide joints needed to keep to course

Short headers

Thin stretchers

Figure 2.2   Brick sizes

12

projects should check with the architect and the quantity surveyor, since enough bricks must be ordered for the landscape walls when the order is placed for the bricks in the main building contract.

Second-hand bricks

Due to the ever increasing cost of bricks, it is sometimes more economical to use second-hand or 'reclaimed' bricks, especially when they are hand-made or very attractive in colour or texture. There are a number of firms who specialize in the reclamation of good facings and there is no reason why they should not be perfectly satisfactory as long as the following points are borne in mind:

- The strength and water absorption of reclaimed bricks is not known, so they should not be used where these attributes are critical.
- Reclaimed bricks should be examined carefully to see that they have not been cracked or chipped by rough handling, as in some cases they have not been dismantled by hand, but have been knocked down with a JCB (a JCB is the all-purpose digger/shovel/excavator used on building sites for everything from digging foundations to lifting the men's tea up onto the scaffolding).
- The supply will be limited, so that the total number of bricks required (plus 10 per cent for wastage) must be ordered at once and the delivery of this quantity must be a binding clause in the contract.
- The old mortar will usually have been lime mortar which is easily cleaned off by gentle tapping. Where a hard cement mortar has been used, however, the reclaimer may have used acid, and this will have had a disastrous effect on the bricks which may not be immediately evident. Acid-cleaned bricks are suspiciously clean and may smell slightly of the chemicals used.
- If possible the provenance of the bricks should be ascertained and the original site inspected to check that the bricks have not been in contact with any damaging material.

Glazed bricks

Some firms manufacture anti-graffiti bricks with an impervious finish, and although these bricks lack the rich texture of natural-surfaced brick, they may be useful in places like car parks and superstores where graffiti are a major problem. The image conveyed by the term 'glazed brick' suggests Victorian institutions, but they can be used very successfully in landscape design. Glazed bricks may be finished in three different ways: with a clay slip fired onto the face of the brick which gives a pottery-type finish; a clear glaze fired onto the face which keeps the original colour but gives an impervious surface; or the traditional glazed brick which can be made in many different colours, including bright reds, greens, blues and white. Such bricks can be used to form patterns or logos on a plain background similar to the earlier London Underground station names. The only problem with these surfaced bricks is that once the surface is damaged by scraping or chipping the whole brick must be cut out and replaced if the surface is to remain vandal-proof.

Engineering bricks

Engineering bricks are very dense, hard, heavy bricks which were originally made for the massive railway, canal, and road civil engineering works of the late nineteenth century. They are made from special clays and are available in two basic colours: a dull red and a deep purple-blue. They are solid bricks with no frog and little or no decorative surface texture, they may be perforated to allow reinforcing rods to be passed through them. Engineering bricks have very sharp arrises and are laid with very thin mortar joints, because since the mortar is less strong than the brick it should only be thick enough to hold the bricks together, and with a sharp arris the full surface of the brick is bedded on the course below.

Engineering bricks are extremely durable, as can be seen in any railway tunnel, and are resistant to almost every form of attack, although their smooth surface is attractive to graffitists. These bricks are also classified by their structural strength, so that precise structural calculations can be made for retaining and other structural walls. Class A engineering bricks have a minimum crushing strength of 70 N/mm^2 with a maximum water absorption of 4.5 per cent by mass, and Class B bricks have a minimum crushing strength of 50 N/mm^2 with a maximum absorption of 7 per cent by mass. The structural strength of engineering bricks is not a major factor in landscape design, but their hardwearing properties are useful in areas of heavy use. They are also unfortunately very expensive, and are therefore usually used only as copings or damp courses in walls or where heavy use and severe vandalism are likely. Walls and planters built in mass engineering brickwork (at least two bricks thick) convey a sense of permanence and solidity which can be used to great effect in the design.

Calcium silicate bricks

Calcium silicate may be sand-lime or flint-lime and as these bricks are not made from natural clay, but from an artificial mixture of minerals, this results in very accurately controlled colour and texture, though the standardization gives a rather uniform appearance to the wall, and they have considerably less variation in colour tone than clay bricks. This quality gives a rather monotonous feeling to the wall, and unless this monotony is to be a feature of the design, it may be desirable to obtain interest by relieving the surface of the wall with string courses, corbels, or a plinth (these features are described later). The colours available are similar to those of clay bricks, that is, mostly in the lighter shades of brown, buff, red and grey. The sizes are the same as those of clay bricks; modular bricks 200 × 100 × 75 mm are available but these cannot be combined with the normal-sized bricks and must be used on their own. Calcium silicate bricks to BS 187 are available in six classes of different strengths (see Table 2.3), and they are suitable for most places where clay bricks would be used, but they should never be used for damp-proof courses.

Table 2.3
Calcium silicate bricks

Type	Strength	Location
Class 2 crushing strength	$14.0N/mm^2$	not suitable for walls
Class 3	$20.5N/mm^2$	walls above DPC
Class 4	$27.5N/mm^2$	cappings and copings
Class 5	$34.5N/mm^2$	retaining walls
Class 6	$41.5N/mm^2$	walls below ground
Class 7	$48.5N/mm^2$	walls below ground

The Class 7 calcium silicate bricks are therefore equal in strength to Class B engineering bricks.

Concrete bricks

Concrete bricks are made to comply with BS 6073: Part 1, and are available in commons, facings, and engineering quality similar to clay bricks. They must have a minimum crushing strength of $7 N/mm^2$ and they are usually available in three strengths for construction work; $20 N/mm^2$, $30 N/mm^2$, and $40 N/mm^2$. In addition to the standard brick size, concrete bricks can be obtained in metric modular sizes of 300 × 100 × 100 mm, 200 × 100 × 100 mm, and 200 × 100 × 75 mm. They are definitely very plain in appearance, and the colours available are pale shades of pink, brown, buff, grey and white. Bricks in deep colours are manufactured, but some may have a tendency to fade under strong sunshine, however, the most modern concrete bricks are manufactured with natural aggregates and iron oxide pigments which provide more permanent colouring. Concrete bricks should not be used where there is a danger of sulphate attack unless they have been specially manufactured for this purpose, using sulphate-resisting cement. The many ranges of 'walling' blocks purporting to imitate Cotswold, York, or other natural stones, are really concrete bricks with appropriate colouring and textures added. They do not have to comply with any standard and should not be used for structural work, though they are required by some local planning authorities in Areas of Outstanding Natural Beauty (AONBs) and other protected areas as a substitute for natural stone.

2.4 BRICK DIMENSIONS

There are several sizes of bricks available and the most frequently used is the traditional nineteenth-century brick size which is just right for the brickie's hand. Thinner bricks similar to the Elizabethan type are used in restoration and replica work, and special-size bricks can be made to order, but this is an exceedingly expensive operation and should only be necessary in exceptional cases. The British Standard brick is 215 × 102.5 × 65 mm, but a tolerance of 72 mm over 24 bricks laid end to end is permitted on these sizes. It must be appreciated that as most bricks vary in practice quite considerably in size and true shape, a wall constructed with one part built of undersized bricks and another part built of oversized bricks will look very peculiar. This is another reason for mixing bricks from all pallets at the same time. It is possible to tie the brick manufacturer down to a much smaller tolerance where large quantities of bricks are being supplied by one works, but this accuracy will be reflected in the cost and will involve many more site visits to check all deliveries of bricks *before* they are built in. If a tighter tolerance on brick sizes and shapes is required this requirement must be part of the contract, as the bricks will either have to be specially manufactured or carefully selected at the brickworks. On a large contract it may be possible to visit the brickworks and set aside stacks or pallets of selected bricks for delivery to the site. 'Selected' or 'purpose-made' bricks will be considerably more expensive than standard bricks. (See Figure 2.2)

For the long runs of plain brickwork most often found in landscape walls, the exact size of brick is not critical, but where brickwork is built in small panels, piers, or integrated with engineering structures it is important to check the sizes and shapes of the bricks to be used. Obviously, the larger the brick the thinner the mortar joint will be, and vice versa, so the landscape designer must bear the visual effect of this in mind when selecting bricks. Wherever possible, brickwork should be built to brick dimensions to save cutting (which is expensive and wasteful) and to preserve the bond which gives the wall its character. A 'metric' brick based on a 100 mm module was introduced some years ago, and is available from a few brickmakers, but it is uncomfortably heavy and the difficulty of integrating it with traditional brickwork proved considerable, so that it is now seldom specified. Bricks are laid either as 'stretchers' with the long face exposed, or as 'headers' with the short-end face exposed, or as 'brick-on-edge' with the short-end face exposed, but with its longest dimension vertical. The metric dimensions used in brickwork include half-millimetre figures, but in practice this is simply silly, since not even the most skilled brickie can build a wall to a closer tolerance than plus or minus 5 mm for ordinary bricks and perhaps 3 mm for engineering bricks. Landscape walls are not regarded as highly accurate building work, and if a lesser tolerance than 15 mm is required for long landscape walls or 10 mm for piers and panels this must be specified. Eventually the UK may follow continental practice and deal in centimetres, which are already common usage in the nurseryman's trade. There are four dimensions to bear in mind when designing brickwork, as follows:

1 the 'work size', which is the size of the brick alone and is the average for the brick 'square' laid dry to test the brick sizes. The dimensions are 215 × 103 × 65 mm.
2 the 'co-ordinating size', which is the unit used for calculating runs of brickwork. It is one brick plus one mortar joint 10 mm thick and gives dimensions of:

> 215 + 10 = 225 mm for a stretcher
> 102.5 + 10 = 112.5 mm for a header
> 65 + 10 = 75 mm for brick-on-edge.

These metric dimensions are close to the traditional 9″, 4 ½″, and 3″ imperial brick dimensions. Walls were described as 9″ thick although technically 8 ⅝″ thick and 4 ½″ walls were technically 4 ⅜″ thick. These figures worked well in practice, and although the metric dimensions may appear more accurate the allowance of ⅜″ in calculating overall building dimensions gave a useful tolerance for bricks of varying sizes and irregular shape. Both metric and imperial brickwork dimensions may be safely described as half, one, or one and a half brick size

3 the 'pier size', which is used when both ends of the wall are exposed. It is a multiple of co-ordinating sizes minus one joint; so for a six-brick-wide pier this would be:

> (6 × 225) − 10 = 1340 mm in stretchers, or
> (12 × 112.5) − 10 = 1340 mm in headers, or
> (18 × 75) − 10 = 1340 mm in brick-on-edge

4 the 'panel size' which is used for brickwork with returned ends. It is a multiple of co-ordinating sizes plus one joint; so for a six-brick-wide panel this would be:

> (6 × 225) + 10 = 1360 mm in stretchers, or
> (12 × 112.5) + 10 = 1360 mm in headers, or
> (18 × 75) + 10 = 1360 mm in brick-on-edge

(See Figure 2.2)

Vertical dimensions are based on the brick height of 65 mm plus one 10 mm joint, and are always multiples of this 75 mm dimension. A horizontal layer of brickwork is a course, and the height of brickwork is often specified by the number of courses, so that a twelve-course wall would be 75 × 12 = 900 mm high. This dimension always includes the bedding joint at the base but not the top joint, as this is calculated in the coping dimension. There are tables

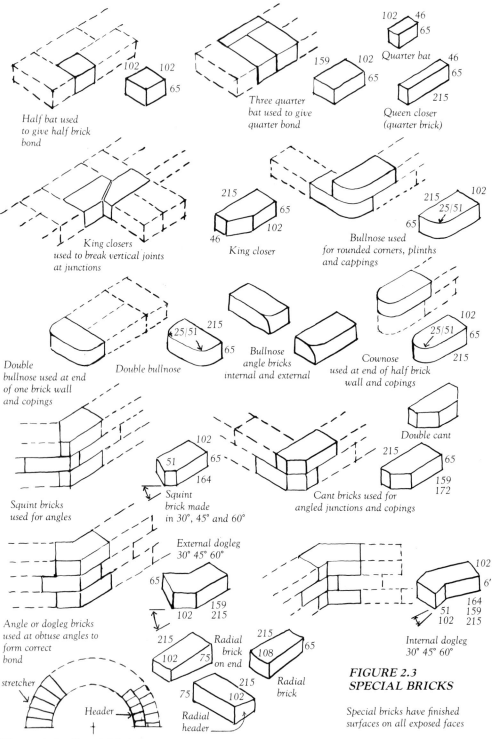

Half bat used
to give half brick
bond

102 102
65

Three quarter
bat used to give
quarter bond

159 102
65

102 46
65

Quarter bat

46
65
215

Queen closer
(quarter brick)

King closers
used to break vertical joints
at junctions

215
65
102
46

King closer

Bullnose used
for rounded corners, plinths
and cappings

215 102
25/51
65

Double
bullnose used at end
of one brick wall
and copings

Double bullnose

25/51 215
65

Bullnose
angle bricks
internal and external

Cownose
used at end of half brick
wall and copings

102
25/51
65
215

Squint bricks
used for angles

102
51 65
164

Squint
brick made
in 30°, 45° and 60°

Cant bricks used for
angled junctions and copings

Double cant

215
65
159
172

Angle or dogleg bricks
used at obtuse angles to
form correct
bond

External dogleg
30° 45° 60°

65
102 159
215

Internal dogleg
30° 45° 60°

102
6'
164
51 159
102 215

stretcher

Header

Radial
brick
on end

215
102 75

215
108 65

Radial
brick

Radial
header

215
75 102

**FIGURE 2.3
SPECIAL BRICKS**

*Special bricks have finished
surfaces on all exposed faces*

Figure 2.3   Special bricks

available for calculating brickwork sizes, but all brickwork is a multiple of the standard sizes, so that calculation is not a difficult matter. For convenience, some co-ordinating sizes (brick and a joint) are given in Table 2.4.

Table 2.4 Brickwork dimensions			
Horizontal		Vertical	
No of bricks	Dimensions	No of courses	Dimensions
½	112.5 mm	1	75mm
1	225.0	2	150
1½	337.5	3	225
2	450.0	4	300
2½	562.5	5	375
3	675.0	6	450
3½	787.5	7	525
4	900.0	8	600
4½	1012.5	9	675
5	1125.0	10	750
5½	1237.5	11	825
6	1350.0	12	900
6½	1462.5	13	975
7	1575.0	14	1050
7½	1687.5	15	1125
8	1800.0	16	1200
8½	1912.5	17	1275
9	2025.0	18	1350
9½	2137.5	19	1425
10	2250.0	20	1500
20	4500.0	24	1800
30	6750.0	28	2100
40	9000.0	32	2400
50	11260.0	36	2700
60	13510.0	40	3000
70	15760.0		

Specials

Traditionally, bricks were cut on site to fit odd corners and angles, but nowadays there are many 'standard specials' which are purpose-made for the job. If only a few specials are needed on the job they are usually cut by the brickie with a sharp tap from a trowel, but hardburnt stocks and expensive handmade facings which do not cut easily should be cut with an angle grinder to avoid waste. (see Figure 2.3) Standard specials are covered by BS 4729 and the most common of these are:

● The snapped header which is a half-bat, and saves wasteful cutting on site when many half-bats are used in the bond.

- The king closer, right- or left-handed, has one corner cut off at a splayed angle, and is used in the more complicated pier and corner bonds to avoid straight vertical joints in the wall.
- The queen closer which is simply a brick split lengthways to give two narrow half-bricks. It is used at the end of a run of quarter bond brick-work to bring the whole course to bond.
- External- and internal-angled corner bricks are now made for those landscape designers who like walls at odd angles and they are usually made in 30°, 45°, and 60° angles.
- Bull-nosed and plinth bricks which are used for string courses, plinths and copings (these are described later).

3 FREESTANDING LANDSCAPE WALLS

This section deals with the construction of the wall and its foundations. A freestanding landscape wall must be stable under all foreseeable weather and site conditions. The main stress on a freestanding wall comes from the pressure exerted by the wind or by the suction on the lee side of the wall, and this pressure needs to be calculated in order to determine the optimum height, thickness and profile of the wall. A map of basic wind speeds for the British Isles is given in *Design of Freestanding Walls*, published by the Brick Development Association, but these are very general. Local wind speed measurements for a period of years should be obtained from the nearest meteorological station, although these figures do not cover the storm-force winds encountered in 1987 and again in 1990. These storms have been regarded as abnormal, but a brief study of any county history shows that equally strong winds are by no means an unusual occurrence, and the landscape designer would be unwise to assume that they are a once-in-a-lifetime event. In addition, the local topography will affect the wind loading, and three categories of topography are recognized; enclosed sheltered landscape or urban landscape; open ground with some windbreak features; and open farm or moorland with no wind deflection. However, in some theoretically sheltered high-rise developments the occasional wind speed may be very high if there is a 'wind-tunnel' effect between high buildings and these must be allowed for in the design. Again, subsequent construction, demolition and even planting may affect the normal wind speeds.

If the average wind speed is known these factors may be applied to it produce a 'design wind pressure' which is used to calculate the estimated wind loading on the wall. When a structural engineer is involved in the design of the building, he may test a model of the site in a wind tunnel to assess the direction and velocity of wind loading on the completed project and these

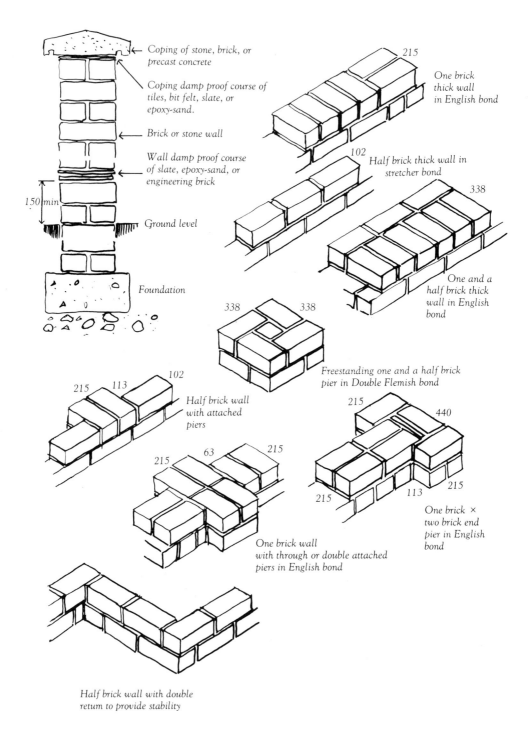

Coping of stone, brick, or precast concrete

Coping damp proof course of tiles, bit felt, slate, or epoxy-sand.

Brick or stone wall

Wall damp proof course of slate, epoxy-sand, or engineering brick

150 min

Ground level

Foundation

215

One brick thick wall in English bond

102

Half brick thick wall in stretcher bond

338

One and a half brick thick wall in English bond

338   338

Freestanding one and a half brick pier in Double Flemish bond

215   113   102

Half brick wall with attached piers

215   63   215

One brick wall with through or double attached piers in English bond

215   440

215   113   215

One brick × two brick end pier in English bond

Half brick wall with double return to provide stability

Figure 3.1   Freestanding landscape walls

22

Table 3.1
Wind speeds

Basic wind speed (from map or local information)	Sheltered site	Partly sheltered site	Exposed site
38 metres/sec	459 N/m^2	572 N/m^2	775 N/m^2
40	509	634	859
42	561	699	947
44	616	767	1040
46	673	838	1136
48	733	912	1237
50	795	990	1343
52	860	1071	1452
54	927	1155	1566
56	997	1242	1684

figures can be used for the landscape walls. The basic wind speed derived from the map will be modified by the nature of the ground and of the surroundings, and Table 3.1 shows a range of basic wind speeds and the consequent wind pressure on a square metre of wall under three different conditions; sheltered by buildings or planting, partly sheltered by wind-breaks or more distant buildings, and completely exposed to the wind force as would be the case in open countryside.

Once the wind loading and any additional pressures caused by turbulence have been determined, the wall thickness, height and profile can be designed. These three factors must be balanced to obtain the most economical and effective wall which will be strong, pleasing to the eye, and effective for its designed purpose. The minimum thickness is determined by the need to resist pressure, though the landscape designer may like to increase the thickness for aesthetic or non-structural reasons such, as the need to match existing walls. The height of walls for calculation purposes is measured from the top of the foundation to the top of the coping. Wall heights are multiples of the standard 75 mm course, and to calculate the full height other dimensions must be added to the visible brick courses, including the brickwork below ground, the coping, the DPC under the coping, and the bottom DPC which is usually an engineering brick or slate course. The depth of brick walls below ground should normally not be more than 225 mm, or two courses, since the effective height of the wall for structural calculations is measured from the top of the foundation, so that the more brickwork there is below ground the greater the effective height of the wall will be. The profile may be a plain straight wall or one of the staggered profiles described below which

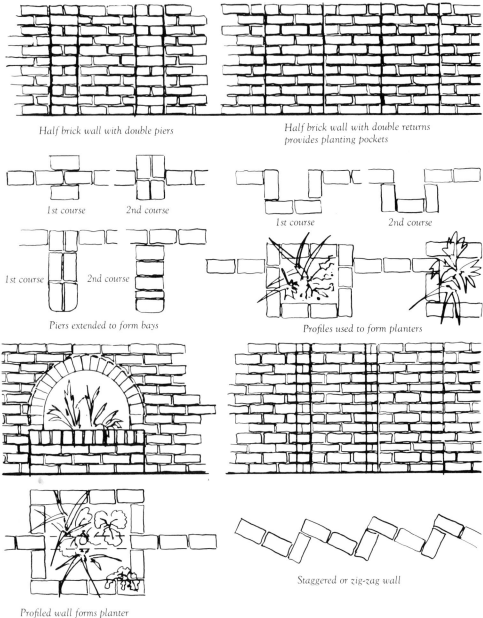

Half brick wall with double piers

Half brick wall with double returns provides planting pockets

1st course   2nd course

1st course   2nd course

1st course   2nd course

Piers extended to form bays

Profiles used to form planters

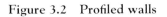

Profiled wall forms planter which stiffens lower third of wall

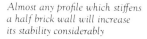

Staggered or zig-zag wall

Stiffening on both sides of the wall provides resistance to wind or other pressure from either side

Almost any profile which stiffens a half brick wall will increase its stability considerably

Figure 3.2   Profiled walls

24

increase the strength of the wall without increasing the thickness. (See Figure 3.1)

3.1   WALL PROFILES

The ability of a wall to resist shocks, subsidence and wind loading may be greatly increased by changing its shape. This may be done in several ways, depending on the character of the project, the height and thickness of the wall and the space available for it. (See Figure 3.2) For example:

- The traditional method of stabilizing long high walls was the buttress, which is a sloping pier built against and into one side of the wall, either vertical or tapering from a projection of three or more bricks at the base to one brick projection within the upper third of the wall.
- Cheaper and less space hungry is the one-sided attached pier, projecting one or two bricks from the wall and continuing vertically up the wall to within the upper third or the full height of the wall to just below the coping. This is satisfactory if pressure is likely to be on one side of the wall only.
- Double-sided attached pier built with a projection of one or two bricks symmetrically on both sides of the wall, giving strength to the wall against pressure from both sides. While wind loading is an obvious source of pressure, the suction generated by strong high winds can be equally destructive and the wall may have to resist considerable suction in a major storm.
- The wall may be stabilized by 'staggering' it, that is, building it in a series of bays with a return into the bay of one, two or three bricks. This feature can be used to enhance planting or to create shelter for delicate plants, and it can also accommodate freestanding or built-in seating.
- The strength of staggering can be increased by making the bay returns one brick thicker than the wall itself.
- If the design of the project permits, the wall can be zig-zagged, which provides rather less stability, shelter, and planting opportunities than the staggered wall. In this case the angles must be designed to present the strongest face to the direction of greatest pressure.
- Serpentine walls can be built using ordinary bricks for curves over 2 m radius, or special radius bricks for smaller curves. They are not easy to integrate into other rectangular features in the landscape design.

Approved profiles

The *Design of Freestanding Walls* discusses some of the types of strengthening described above, and divides them into three categories of wall profile which

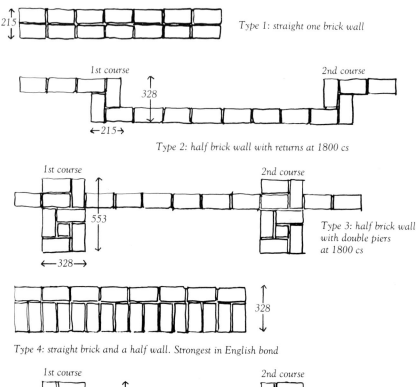

215   Type 1: straight one brick wall

1st course   2nd course

328

←215→

Type 2: half brick wall with returns at 1800 cs

1st course   2nd course

553

←328→

Type 3: half brick wall
with double piers
at 1800 cs

328

Type 4: straight brick and a half wall. Strongest in English bond

1st course   2nd course

665

←328→

Type 7:
straight half brick wall
with double sided piers
at 1800 cs.

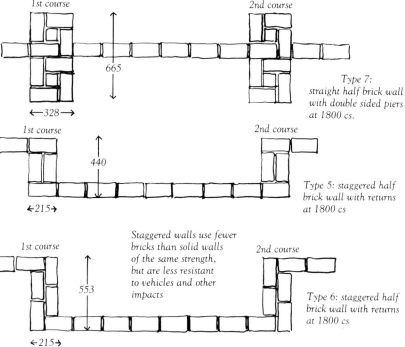

1st course   2nd course

440

←215→

Type 5: staggered half
brick wall with returns
at 1800 cs

Staggered walls use fewer
bricks than solid walls
of the same strength,
but are less resistant
to vehicles and other
impacts

1st course   2nd course

553

←215→

Type 6: staggered half
brick wall with returns
at 1800 cs

Figure 3.3   GLC approved profiles

Plate 2   Staggered wall   *A staggered patttern of wall designed to increase the stability of a comparatively slender wall. This is one of the methods used to stiffen a thin wall without increasing the thickness of the brickwork.*

can be used to increase the strength of a wall, as detailed in Table 3.2. (See also Figure 3.3)

Calculations

Naturally, the dimensions given in Table 3.2 can be modified to suit the landscape design, but the structural principles should be maintained in all cases, and if there is a considerable variation, the full calculations given in the publication will have to be made. The bays of 1800 mm are the widest that can be allowed without the necessity of separate calculations for the bay wall, as the pressure in the centre of an overlong bay can exceed the design load even though the wall as a whole is sufficiently strong. Recommended maximum loadings are given for these types of wall, but as the safety factor ranges from 3.1 to 3.5, and the real wind loadings, quality of bricklaying, the strength of the actual bricks used and the quality of the mortar are all

---

Table 3.2
Wall profiles

Types 1, 2 and 3 (the weakest)

Type 1 is a straight one-brick wall without piers or returns
Type 2 is a staggered GLC pattern half-brick wall with returns 215 × 328 mm at 1800 mm centres
Type 3 is a straight half-brick wall with double-sided piers 328 × 553 mm at 1800 mm centres

Types 5 and 7 (medium strength)

Type 5 is a staggered half-brick wall with returns 215 × 440 mm at 1800 mm centres
Type 7 is a straight half-brick wall with double-sided piers 328 × 665 mm at 1800 mm centres

Types 4 and 6 (the strongest)

Type 4 is a straight brick and a half wall without piers or returns
Type 6 is a staggered GLC pattern half brick wall with returns 215 × 553 mm at 1800 mm centres

---

imprecise in practice, these figures can be regarded as guidelines rather than as true structural calculations. If the wall is in an unusual or complicated situation, the services of a structural engineer should be employed and the selection of the bricks and the bricklaying will require more care.

As a guide to the landscape designer, Table 3.3 gives the maximum pressure loadings for a typical wall in each of the three categories listed in Table 3.2. The figures have been interpolated from the published graph for a range of wall heights up to 3000 mm, using the larger permissible safety factor of 3.5 (some local authorities will allow a safety factor of 3.1). It is assumed that the loading will be evenly distributed over the whole face of the wall and that no point loads (which would have to be calculated separately) will be applied. This typical wall consists of two parts: the plain brickwork from ground level to the coping DPC and the top and base of the wall which comprise 225 mm of brickwork below ground, 15 mm of slate DPC, a 10 mm top mortar joint, 5 mm DPC under the coping, and a brick-on-edge coping 103 mm high, giving a total figure of 358 mm to be added to the plain brickwork.

Using the table of wind speeds (Table 3.1) and the figures given in Table 3.3 the landscape designer could design a wall 2008 mm high of type 4 (a straight one-and-a-half-brick wall) which would withstand a pressure of 1085 N/m², generated by a normal wind speed of 44 m/second on an open site, and up to 52 m/sec on a partly sheltered site. Alternatively, he could use a type 7 wall (half-brick thick with double piers) for the same situation, but it could only be 1708 mm high. The landscape designer can therefore choose between a thin staggered wall or a thick straight wall or a combination of both. In addition to the normal wind loads, extra stresses on the wall can be caused by hanging solid gates on the wall, and these extra loads will have to be calculated unless the wall is reinforced by piers. Weak points in walls occur where movement joints are not strengthened by piers, and where panels of thin brickwork have been allowed to exceed the 1800 mm safe limit.

Table 3.3
Permissible wall heights

Full wall height			Wall types 1,2,3	Wall types 5 and 7	Wall types 4 and 6
358 +	1200 mm =	1558 mm	730 N/m²	1255 N'm²	1685 N/m²
	1350	1708	615	1065	1430
	1500	1858	535	920	1235
	1650	2008	470	810	1085
	1800	2158	410	720	970
	1950	2308		635	855
	2100	2458		580	785
	2250	2608		520	700
	2400	2758		475	622
	2550	2908		435	590
	2700	3058		408	545
	2850	3208			508
	3000	3358			470

3.2 FOUNDATIONS

The foundations are essential to the sound construction of the wall. They must be capable of taking all the weight of the wall and its piers plus any superimposed loading contributed by people or structures such as pergolas. The function of the foundation is to distribute the load of the wall evenly and safely over the ground below it, whatever the bearing capacity of the ground may be.

Walls may have to be built along a line which crosses several substrates of different bearing capabilities; part may be fill, part natural ground, and part existing roadways or hard standings, and it will be necessary to determine the correct type of foundation for each case. In very soft ground such as made-up soil, peaty ground, or ground of unknown consistency, foundations should be taken down to good bearing ground, or reinforced. Foundations may be reinforced by placing light welded-rod mesh similar to that used for brickwork reinforcement at the top and bottom of the foundation slab. The steel should be covered by at least 50 mm of concrete top and bottom. Where there is a sharp change in the bearing capacity along the line of the wall it will be necessary to provide movement joints in the foundation and also in the wall above so that differential settlement can be taken up without cracking or distortion of the wall. Where walls are stepped the foundation usually follows the stepping and an overlap of 300 mm or twice the thickness of the foundation (whichever is the greater) should be provided. In cohesive soils such as dry stiff clay, the foundation trench may be left as dug, but in soft clay, loose gravel or sand, and soft chalk, the bottom of the trench should be filled with 100 mm of well-rammed hardcore and 'blinded' (the crevices filled) with sand before laying the foundation.

There are three dangers affecting shallow foundations for heavy walls: frost, shrinkage, and trees. Frost heave may cause lifting of the foundation slab. A depth below ground of 450 mm will provide protection in most areas of the British Isles; though any increase in depth of foundations will affect the 'effective height' of the wall when calculations as to its stability are being made. Shrinkage can be a serious problem in areas of shrinkable clays, notably the London region, and a depth of 900 mm may be needed to avoid this risk. Excavation close to the foundations, addition or removal of land drains, and site de-watering may all cause shrinkage or expansion of clay soils, so that ground which was sound at the time of the site investigation may become unstable as a result of these works. If water is naturally or artificially present close to the wall it may be necessary to lay land drains to control the water. Walls built on slopes of mixed formation may be subjected to straight or rotational ground slip which can be exacerbated by the construction of the wall. Mature trees are capable of drawing water from depths of 5 m and in seasons of drought this may cause shrinkage. In any of these circumstances it is better to play safe and to increase the depth and thickness of the foundation slab over the minimum required by structural calculations rather than to risk settlement and cracking which is difficult and expensive to remedy.

The average permissible bearing pressures for different types of soil are detailed in Table 3.4.

If the wall is not a standard type or if the stability of the ground is dubious, the foundations should be calculated in accordance with the formulae given in *Design of Freestanding Walls*, or BS 5628, but if there is any incomprehensible abnormality about the expected stresses on the wall or the bearing capacity of the ground, it is advisable to employ a structural engineer to prepare full calculations. Although calculations may result in narrow strip foundations, the contractor needs 450 mm width for the brickie to work below ground level or for mechanical diggers and 300 mm width for shovels, so that these will always be the minimum widths of strip foundations regardless of calculations. Remember that it is often necessary to make the foundation itself deeper than the minimum 300 mm in order to reach good ground, and when in doubt, choose a foundation larger than the minimum, since concrete is cheaper than claims for professional negligence. Table 3.5 gives typical foundations for the wall profiles discussed above.

Table 3.4
Bearing pressures of substrates

Group	Soils	Allowable bearing pressure kN/m^2
I	granite	10000
	limestone, sandstone	4000
	hard shale, soft sandstone	2000
	clay shale	1000
	solid chalk	600
	broken strata, soft chalk	assess
II	compact gravel	600*
	dense gravel, sand/gravel	200–600*
	loose gravel, sand/gravel	200*
	compact sand	300*
	dense sand	100–300*
	loose sand	less than 100*
III	hard clay	300–600
	stiff clay	150–300
	firm clay	75–150
	soft clay and silt	75
	soft clay, soft silt	less than 75
IV	peat	foundations to be taken down below organic soil
V	land fill	assess, and reinforce foundation slab

*These figures are for dry soil

Concrete for foundations

The concrete for wall foundations should be to BS 5328, and not less in strength than the prescribed mix C7.5P with 40 mm max. aggregate, which is roughly equivalent to the traditional 1:3:6 (cement: sand: coarse aggregate) mix, or a1:8 all-in (cement: sand and aggregate combined). This latter is a less accurate mix but quite adequate for non-structural walls. For structural wall foundations or very wet site conditions it is better to use prescribed mix C10P with 20 mm max. aggregate, which is roughly equivalent to 1:2 ½:5 (cement: sand: coarse aggregate) mix or 1:6 all-in (cement: sand and aggregate combined). A very large proportion of construction concrete is supplied as 'ready-mixed' to one of the British Standard specifications and most of it comes from accredited suppliers who comply with the Quality Scheme for Ready Mixed Concrete (QSRMC) which guarantees the quality. Unless otherwise specified, the cement used is ordinary Portland cement (OPC)

Table 3.5
Typical foundation dimensions

Wall type	Maximum height (mm)	Width of foundation (mm)			Thickness of foundation (mm)	Depth to base of foundation (mm)
		50 kN/m²	100 kN/m²	150 kN/m²		
Type 1	2250	500	500	500	300	500
Type 2	2250	500	500	500	300	500
		includes 215 mm return				
Type 3:						
wall	2250	500	500	500	300	500
piers		447	197	197	300	500
		wider than piers				
Type 4	3250	800	600	500	300	500–750
Type 5	3000	600	600	600	400	500–750
		includes 337 mm return				
Type 6	3250	700	700	700	500	500–750
		includes 450 mm return				
Type 7:						
wall	3000	500	500	500	300	500–750
piers		535	135	135	300	500–750
		wider than piers				

which is suitable for most sites, but where site investigation indicates a possibility of sulphate attack, sulphate resisting Portland cement (OPSRC) should be specified. Sand, or 'fine aggregate' is material which passes a 5 mm sieve. It is controlled by BS 882 and should be clean sharp washed pit or river sand – not sea sand unless it has been thoroughly washed. Good sand should have no earth or organic matter in it, and it should fall away cleanly from the hand when squeezed without leaving any residue or staining. Coarse aggregate, usually specified as 20 mm maximum (or 40 mm maximum for large and deep foundations), is also controlled by BS 882. It may be graded mixed gravels and shingle, or broken hard rock without dust, but not broken concrete or brick. It should be free from earth, oil, old rubber boots or other pollutants and graded evenly from fine to coarse. Good aggregate does not break up when handled and must be rounded, not jagged as otherwise air pockets may be left in the concrete. 'All-in' aggregate which combines fine and coarse aggregate, should be properly graded from sand particle size to 20 mm aggregate (or as specified) without dust. It may be mixed in the builder's yard, or it may 'as dug' ballast which is a natural mix of aggregate straight from the pit.

Concrete sets by means of a chemical reaction between the cement and the mixing water and this reaction begins as soon as the water is added. The fully mixed concrete will remain workable for about two hours after mixing – more on cold damp days and less on dry hot days – and it must never on any account be 'knocked up'; that is, made workable again by the addition of more water. The workable period may be prolonged by the addition of 'retarders'; chemicals which delay the setting time, but these additions should not be necessary unless the mixed concrete has to be transported long distances after mixing. Ready-mixed concrete which comes by truck from the mixing firm has retarders added to allow for the journey time. Concrete takes up its initial set quite quickly, but only one third of its strength has developed after seven days, and it does not reach its designed strength until twenty-eight days after pouring.

Concrete for structural walls and their foundations, especially reinforced concrete, is controlled by many British Standards or Codes of Practice and trade standards which deal in detail with the chemical analysis of all materials, their exact weights and densities, and very careful control of mixing and placing on site, but the landscape designer need not demand the same stringent level of control over the concrete for freestanding wall foundations, since there is little risk of structural collapse due to faulty concrete. For example, structural concrete must not be tipped into shuttering from a height, since the aggregate may settle out under the impact, but obviously this is not important in a foundation 300 mm thick. If the landscape contract is part of a building contract concrete can be obtained from the main contractor's suppliers, but on isolated jobs the concrete may be supplied as ready-mix or may even have to be mixed on site. With a large batch mixer, the concrete is mixed by weight, which is more accurate, but for small mixers and hand mixing, the proportions are mixed by volume. If the concrete is being mixed on site in small quantities, the following points should be checked; admittedly they are legally the responsibility of the contractor, but the landscape designer should satisfy himself that good practice is being followed:

- The mixer must be clean at the start of mixing, and must not contain the remains of the last batch, which will affect the setting time.
- The water used must be clean and of drinking quality.
- The cement must be kept completely dry on site and in transit, and should be used within two weeks of manufacture, since up to 20 per cent of strength can be lost after four to six weeks. Cement supplied directly to the site by a reputable builder's merchant will be fresh. It is, however, very tempting for the main contractor to use up old cement which has been lying about in his yard on landscape work, but this should never be permitted.
- The aggregate must be stored on a clean hard surface and not on the ground.
- The order of mixing must be (1) half the water and half the aggregate in

33

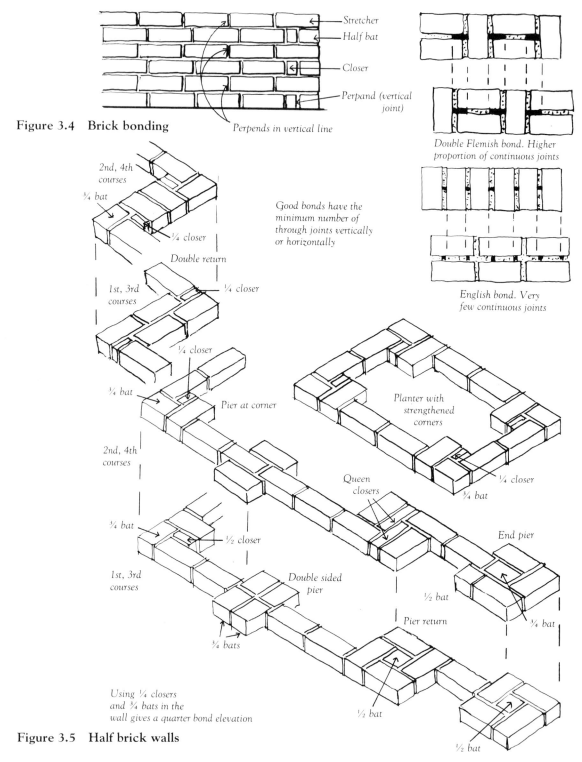

Figure 3.4 Brick bonding

Stretcher

Half bat

Closer

Perpand (vertical joint)

Perpends in vertical line

Double Flemish bond. Higher proportion of continuous joints

English bond. Very few continuous joints

Good bonds have the minimum number of through joints vertically or horizontally

2nd, 4th courses

¾ bat

¼ closer

Double return

1st, 3rd courses

¼ closer

¼ closer

¾ bat

¼ closer

Pier at corner

Planter with strengthened corners

¼ closer

¾ bat

2nd, 4th courses

Queen closers

¾ bat

½ closer

End pier

1st, 3rd courses

Double sided pier

½ bat

¾ bat

¾ bats

Pier return

½ bat

Using ¼ closers and ¾ bats in the wall gives a quarter bond elevation

½ bat

Figure 3.5 Half brick walls

the drum (2) most of the cement and sand (3) remainder of the materials alternately (4) mix for three minutes.

- The concrete should be compacted into the foundation trench, but not so much that the cement rises to the surface.
- If the foundation trench is in soft ground, care must be taken to avoid loose soil falling into the concrete.
- Newly poured foundations need protection in hot dry weather to prevent the water necessary for curing from drying out. They also need protection in frost conditions, but as the sides are protected by the sides of the trench only the top surface is vulnerable to heat or cold.
- Sand may have a moisture content varying from 5 per cent to 15 per cent, and wet sand should be left piled for 24 hours before using in order to drain surplus water.
- The concretor should use a 'gauge box' which is a bottomless wooden box filled with the dry aggregate or cement and struck level, so that the proportions are accurately measured. Materials measured by the 'small shovelful' or 'half a bucket' do not produce good concrete.

For those landscape designers who would like to learn more about concrete, the British Cement Association (BCA) publications *Introduction to Concrete* and *Concrete mixes for General Purposes* will be useful; for concrete handling on site, the BCA publish a series of *Man on the Job* booklets which give excellent advice on concrete control.

3.3   BRICKWORK BONDS

The main purpose of bonding brickwork is to achieve the maximum strength and stability compatible with the minimum of cutting. Bonds are also designed to give different textures to a wall such as evenness, and vertical or horizontal emphasis, and with those types of brick whose headers are of a different shade to the stretcher face some interesting patterns can be obtained. The diagonal patterns seen in East Anglia are derived from the eighteenth-century Dutch influence and are sometimes called Dutch bonds in consequence. (See Figure 3.4)

Sometimes, landscape designers specify a half-brick wall to be laid fairface both sides: this is not really possible since the variation in brick sizes makes it impossible to get *both* faces into true planes. A one-brick wall is the minimum thickness which can be laid with two more or less fair faces, and for truly accurate fairface work on *both* sides, a brick-and-a-half-thick wall is necessary. If a really first-class finish is required to both faces of the wall, the specification must include a clause forbidding 'over-hand' working, where the brickie works from one side of the wall only, in order to save the cost of double scaffolding, and consequently he cannot see the other side of the wall as he lays it. The correct bonding of quoins, junctions, piers and pilasters is of great importance, both for structural strength, and because these parts of the wall catch the eye most frequently. It is not unusual to see the ends of landscape walls broken or cracked, even where traffic has not caused the damage, and this is most likely to be due to careless bonding or insufficient stability caused by trying to economize on the size of piers and returns.

Half-brick walls

The commonest bond used is the simple and rather dull stretcher bond, where all the bricks are laid as stretchers with evenly staggered perpends, and it should be used for half-brick-thick walls only. In a half-brick wall the appearance of stretcher bond can be improved by using quarter bond, that is, staggering the perpends a quarter-brick apart rather than a half-brick apart; this gives a slight vertical stripe to the brickwork. Another change in appearance can be made by using raking bond, where each course is staggered a quarter-brick to the left of the one below; this gives a diagonal striped effect to the wall. Both these patterns can be emphasized by careful selection of mortar joints. Snapped header or special half-brick bats may also be used in a half-brick wall to give a more interesting bond, but this is more expensive than using stretchers only, and where funds permit it is better to build a one-brick-thick wall if a bond with headers is desired. A further version of half-brick walling is the honeycomb bond in which the bricks are spaced out to give an open grid with a view through the wall. It has little or no strength, and should only be used for small decorative walls where no rough treatment is expected. It is very suitable for low screening walls or for small panels in larger solid walls where glimpses of landscape without access are desirable. They are easily vandalized and should not be used in areas where they may be subjected to abuse. (See Figure 3.11)

One-brick walls and thicker walls

The main structural wall bonds used in building work are Double Flemish bond and English bond. These are used for walls subject to structural stresses in walls one, one-and-a-half, and two-bricks thick. Current low cost practice is to build in 'collar bond', which consists of two vertical skins of half-bricks in stretcher bond tied together with wire ties. This deplorable method should never be used as it relies for its strength entirely on the mortar joint between the two skins and the regular spacing of ties, neither of which can be checked visually on site by the landscape designer. The use of substandard mortar and careless wall-tie placing, which may occur even with good site inspection, is a guarantee of eventual disaster, particularly since there is some disquiet in the construction industry over the use of wall ties for holding two skins of brickwork together due to potential corrosion. Housing is especially at risk, as some of the older buildings with the cavity walls dictated by Building Regulations are now suffering from corrosion of the ties and consequent loss

Plate 3   Honeycomb brickwork   *A half brick wall in honeycomb bond. This wall allows air and light to pass through the wall while still providing some privacy. It is vulnerable to vandalism or accidental damage, and is best suited to quiet pedestrian areas.*

of structural stability. It seems unwise to rely on unproven methods of construction when good permanent brick bonding has been satisfactory for many generations. Traditionally, brick walls were constructed five or six bricks thick, but nowadays these are not likely to arise in landscape work, though if they are specified for aesthetic or practical reasons the bonding principles already established for thinner walls are carried on throughout the wall thickness. The calculations for landscape walls take no account of the bond used as a factor in determining strength, but where there is likely to be

37

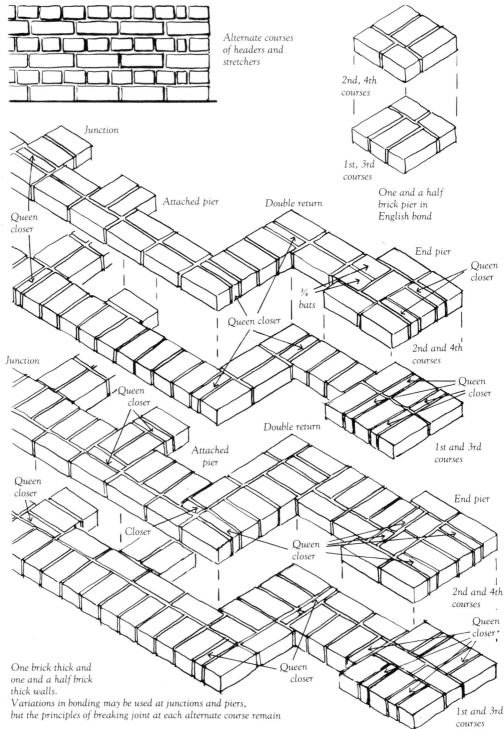

Alternate courses of headers and stretchers

2nd, 4th courses

1st, 3rd courses

One and a half brick pier in English bond

Junction

Queen closer

Attached pier

Double return

Queen closer

¾ bats

End pier

Queen closer

2nd and 4th courses

Junction

Queen closer

Queen closer

Attached pier

Double return

Queen closer

Queen closer

1st and 3rd courses

Queen closer

Closer

End pier

Queen closer

2nd and 4th courses

Queen closer

Queen closer

1st and 3rd courses

One brick thick and one and a half brick thick walls.
Variations in bonding may be used at junctions and piers, but the principles of breaking joint at each alternate course remain

Figure 3.6   English bond

38

considerable stress on the wall it is better to use either English or Double Flemish bond rather than one of the Garden Wall bonds.

English bond

This is the strongest unreinforced brick bond. It is built with alternate courses of headers and stretchers, and gives a regular pattern with very even texture. It has the advantage that there are no straight vertical joints in the wall, and is therefore very stable (see Figure 3.6).

Double Flemish bond

It is not clear where the name 'Flemish' comes from, but presumably the bond was imported from the Low Countries when the building boom supported by the wool trade between England and Flanders was at its height. It is aesthetically one of the most attractive bonds, and is built with alternate headers and stretchers in each course, with a header centrally over each stretcher. This bond has a number of straight vertical joints in its composition, and is therefore less strong than English bond, but unless the wall is stressed this factor is not important. Flemish bond may be strengthened by inserting a course of three headers and one stretcher every three or five courses, but care should be taken that this does not spoil the appearance of the wall, as if the wall is less than twelve courses high this will look like a mistake in bonding rather than an intentional variation (see Figure 3.7).

Single Flemish bond

This can only be used in one-and-a-half brick or thicker walls, where Flemish bond is used on the face with English bond at the rear. Although this does save on expensive facings it is only worthwhile where very costly handmade bricks are being used, since the brickie must work with two types of brick at once and these may vary considerably in size. The complexity of this work will certainly be reflected in the labour costs (See Figure 3.8).

Garden Wall bonds

As the name indicates, these bonds were originally developed for walls enclosing parks and herb and kitchen gardens where structural strength is less important than in building work; garden walls were also more likely to be built by semi-skilled labour from the landowner's estate rather than by skilled craftsmen. They are simpler in design than English and Flemish bonds, but they are perfectly sound bonds, although they should not be used where the wall may be subjected to stress.

English Garden Wall bond

This is another aesthetically attractive bond which has a sequence of one course of headers and three courses of stretchers, giving a pronounced horizontal pattern to the wall which may be useful to the landscape designer.

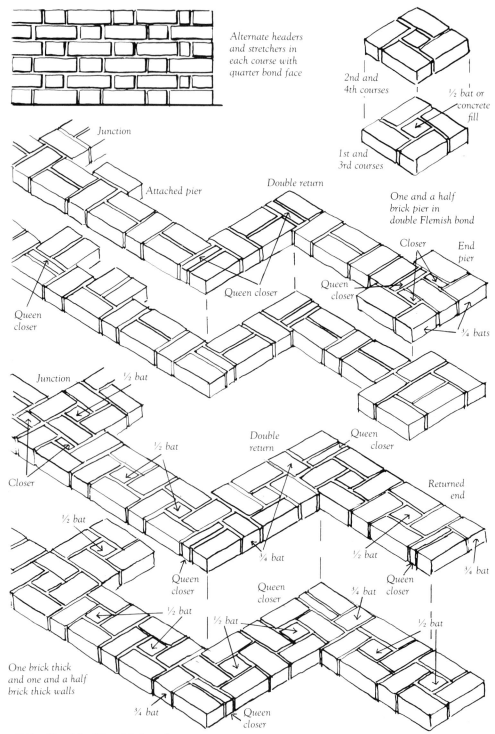

Alternate headers and stretchers in each course with quarter bond face

2nd and 4th courses

1st and 3rd courses

½ bat or concrete fill

Junction

Attached pier

Double return

One and a half brick pier in double Flemish bond

Queen closer

Closer

End pier

Queen closer

Queen closer

¾ bats

Junction

½ bat

½ bat

Double return

Queen closer

Returned end

Closer

½ bat

¾ bat

½ bat

¾ bat

½ bat

Queen closer

Queen closer

Queen closer

¾ bat

Queen closer

½ bat

½ bat

½ bat

One brick thick and one and a half brick thick walls

¾ bat

Queen closer

Figure 3.7   Double Flemish bond

40

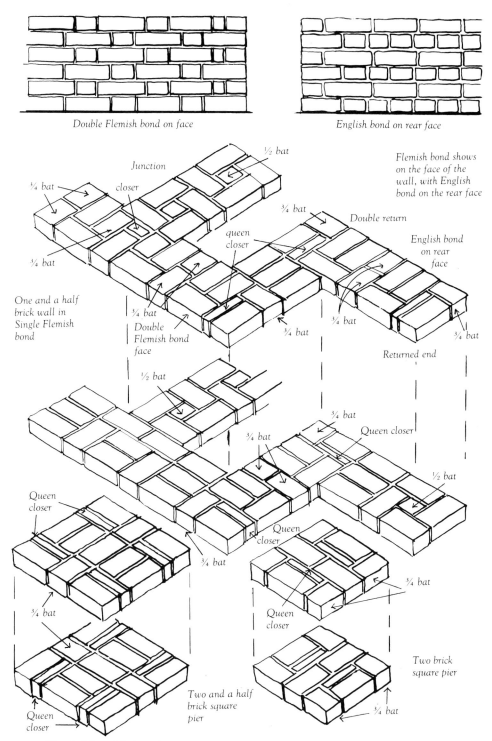

Double Flemish bond on face

English bond on rear face

Flemish bond shows
on the face of the
wall, with English
bond on the rear face

Junction

½ bat

¾ bat

closer

¾ bat

queen
closer

¾ bat

Double return

English bond
on rear
face

¾ bat

One and a half
brick wall in
Single Flemish
bond

¾ bat
Double
Flemish bond
face

¾ bat

¾ bat

¾ bat

Returned end

½ bat

¾ bat

Queen closer

¾ bat

½ bat

Queen
closer

Queen
closer

¾ bat

Queen
closer

¾ bat

Queen
closer

Two brick
square pier

¾ bat

Queen
closer

Two and a half
brick square
pier

¾ bat

Figure 3.8   Single Flemish bond

41

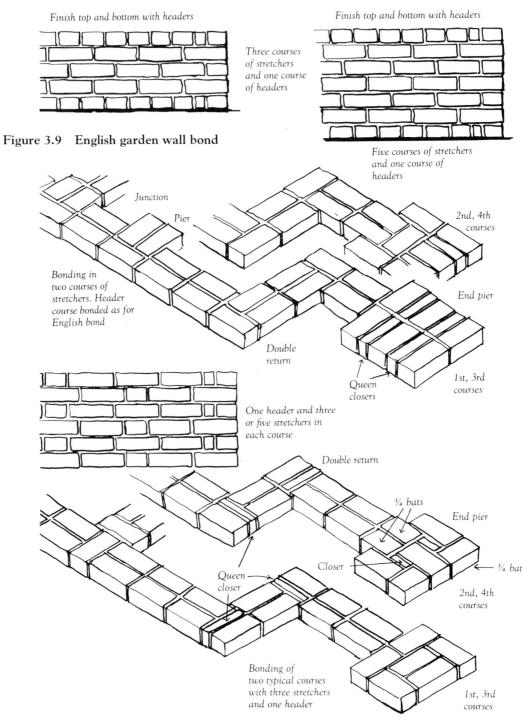

Finish top and bottom with headers

Three courses
of stretchers
and one course
of headers

Finish top and bottom with headers

Figure 3.9   English garden wall bond

Five courses of stretchers
and one course of
headers

Junction

Pier

2nd, 4th
courses

Bonding in
two courses of
stretchers. Header
course bonded as for
English bond

End pier

Double
return

Queen
closers

1st, 3rd
courses

One header and three
or five stretchers in
each course

Double return

¾ bats

End pier

Closer

¾ bat

Queen
closer

2nd, 4th
courses

Bonding of
two typical courses
with three stretchers
and one header

1st, 3rd
courses

Figure 3.10   Flemish garden wall bond

42

All garden wall bonds contain a high proportion of stretchers which mean long straight joints in the centre of the wall, thus reducing the strength of the wall, though this is not an important consideration for low walls. The use of headers in a separate course enables them to be used for emphasizing the horizontal character, especially if they are of a different shade to the stretchers. If a stronger horizontal emphasis is desired the stretcher joints can be kept to the minimum so that the headers will project slightly to form a string course (See Figure 3.9).

Flemish garden wall bond

This is one of the most suitable bonds for landscape walls as it is simple to lay and uses the minimum number of headers, which makes it easier to get a fair face both sides, and it has a pleasing appearance. Each course consists of three stretchers and one header, staggered so that the headers form vertical lines. This bond also makes good use of bricks with different tones on header and stretcher faces, and for a stronger emphasis, different coloured bricks may be used for headers and stretchers (See Figure 3.10).

Sometimes five courses of stretchers and one course of headers are used instead of three courses of stretchers in both English and Flemish Garden Wall bonds, and even seven courses have been known, but this practice is undesirable because it results in a comparatively weak structure.

Rat-trap bond

This is similar to Flemish Garden Wall bond, but the bricks are laid on edge making each course 112.5 mm high with a gap in the middle of the wall between the stretchers on each face. It has little strength, but saves a considerable number of bricks and can be used for low boundary walls where cost is important and no strain is placed on the wall.

Rat-trap bond is also used as a framework for a strongly reinforced wall where a brick face is required but where plain brickwork would not be strong enough. The wall is reinforced by passing steel rods through the central space and concreting them in. When rat-trap bond is used in this way it is called 'Quetta' bond, after the Indian city where it was presumably first used (See Figure 3.11).

3.4   ANGLES AND CURVES

All the bonds described above are capable of being carried round acute, obtuse or curved lines on plan. It is very tempting to make a series of dwarf walls more interesting by including circles, triangles and other shapes in the design, but even with the help of special bricks these features will be much more expensive than straight and rectangular designs. Such angles and curves are also more vulnerable than plain brickwork to damage and will cost more

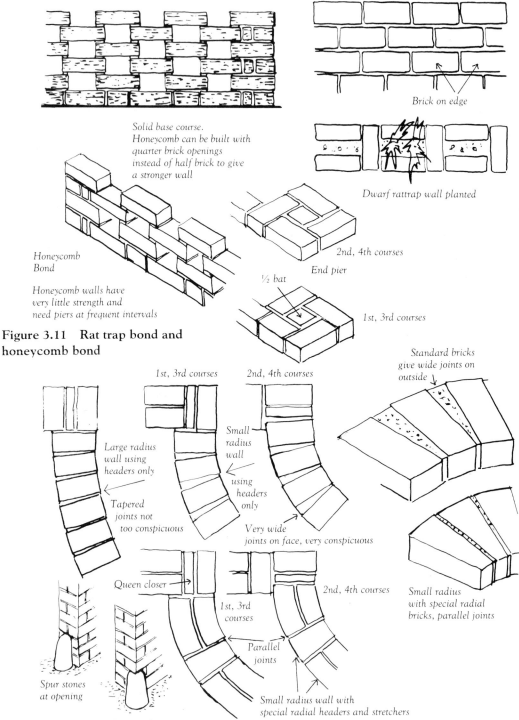

Solid base course.
Honeycomb can be built with
quarter brick openings
instead of half brick to give
a stronger wall

Brick on edge

Dwarf rattrap wall planted

Honeycomb
Bond

Honeycomb walls have
very little strength and
need piers at frequent intervals

2nd, 4th courses

End pier

½ bat

1st, 3rd courses

**Figure 3.11   Rat trap bond and
honeycomb bond**

1st, 3rd courses

2nd, 4th courses

Standard bricks
give wide joints on
outside

Large radius
wall using
headers only

Small
radius
wall

Tapered
joints not
too conspicuous

using
headers
only

Very wide
joints on face, very conspicuous

Small radius
with special radial
bricks, parallel joints

Queen closer

1st, 3rd
courses

2nd, 4th courses

Parallel
joints

Spur stones
at opening

Small radius wall with
special radial headers and stretchers

Figure 3.12a   Angles and curves

44

Plate 4 Garden wall   *An interesting traditional garden wall in a brickmaking district. The overburnt and deformed bricks are used to construct a random textured surface which looks dark and rough, forming a good background for vegetation. It is extremely durable, but it is most suitable for an informal landscape. These bricks are not so common as they were when bricks were clamp burnt, but they may still be found occasionally.*

to repair, so that they ought to be used with restraint unless they are an essential component of the design (See Figures 3.12a–g).

Angles, ends, or openings in a wall are likely to be damaged by vehicles, including small wheeled objects such as bicycles, wheelbarrows, shopping trolleys, and mowing machines. At these points the landscape designer should allow room to erect spur stones to protect the brickwork. These were traditionally used to prevent the wheels of carts, waggons, and coaches from scarring and eventually destroying the brickwork if the driver turned short when entering the opening. Although waggons had iron-shod wheels capable of shattering soft stone or brick, even modern machinery can do a lot of damage unless restricted by some form of protection. It is possible to use heavy timbers or rolled-steel angles to protect corners, similar to those used in industrial estates, but they are not attractive and it is preferable to use purpose-made precast concrete spur stones set against the end of the brick-

45

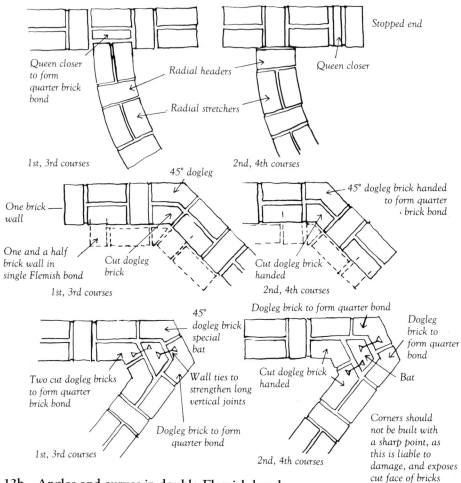

Figure 3.12b   Angles and curves in double Flemish bond

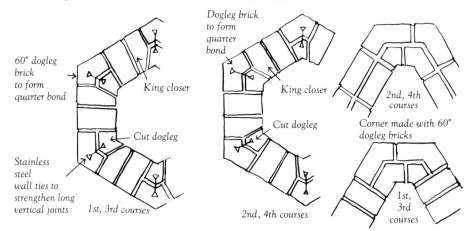

Figure 3.12c   Header bond

46

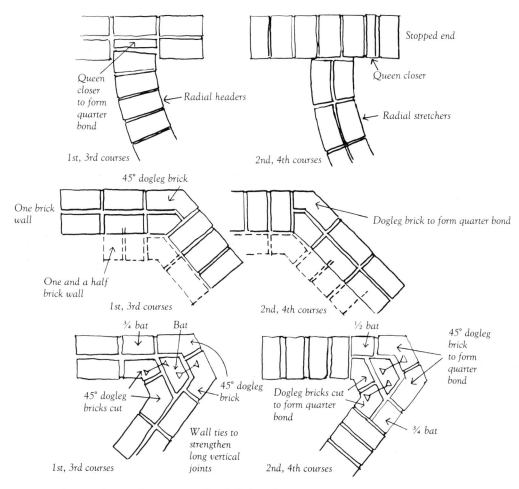

Figure 3.12d Angles and curves in English bond

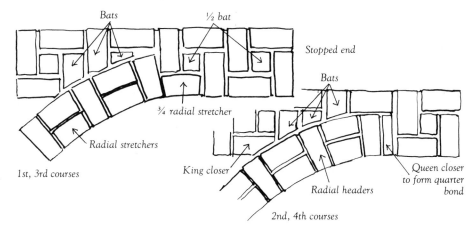

Figure 3.12e Junction of curved and straight walls in double Flemish bond

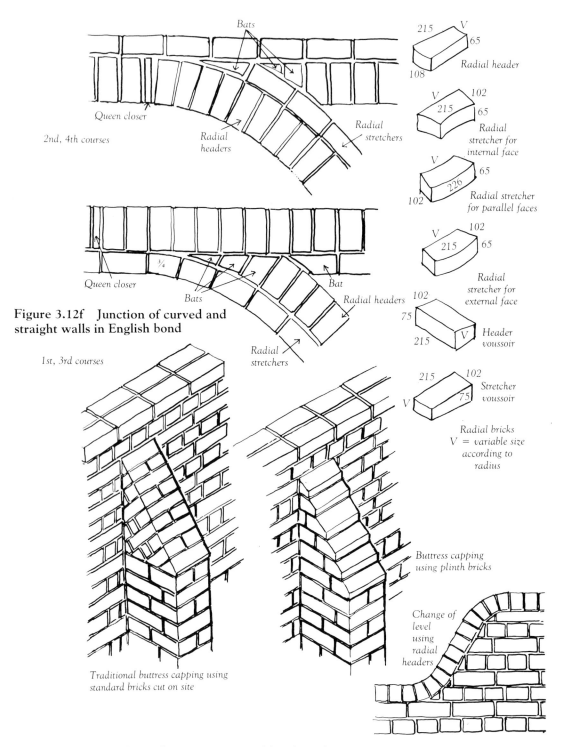

215 V
65
108
Radial header

V 102
215 65
Radial stretcher for internal face

V 65
226
102
Radial stretcher for parallel faces

V 102
215 65
Radial stretcher for external face

102
75
215 V
Header voussoir

215 102
75
V
Stretcher voussoir

Radial bricks
V = variable size according to radius

Bats

Queen closer

2nd, 4th courses

Radial headers

Radial stretchers

Queen closer

¾

Bats

Bat

Radial headers

Figure 3.12f Junction of curved and straight walls in English bond

Radial stretchers

1st, 3rd courses

Buttress capping using plinth bricks

Change of level using radial headers

Traditional buttress capping using standard bricks cut on site

Figure 3.12g   Angles and curves in vertical brickwork

work. They are made with flat backs, half-round in plan, or quadrant-shaped to fit over a wall angle, and are about 500 mm high which protects the wall against most wheels, and the width of the opening must be designed to allow for them. The landscape designer should consult his client to ascertain whether any special protection is needed for that particular site.

3.5   MOVEMENT JOINTS

All brickwork moves to a greater or lesser extent. There are two kinds of movement which must be considered by the landscape designer; lateral movement caused by the contraction and expansion of the brickwork itself due to temperature and weather conditions, and the vertical movement caused by differential settlement between one part of the wall and the other. The average movement which may be expected to occur from thermal expansion or ground consolidation is 1 mm per metre run, and the movement joint should allow for this (See Figure 3.13).

Lateral expansion joints

Lateral movement joints should be provided at maximum intervals of 15 m in long walls and the width of the movement joint should be 1 mm per metre of wall. Obviously these joints should be made at points where they can best be accommodated in the design; at junctions, behind piers, or where they can be made a feature of the design. Lateral expansion and contraction joints are not taken down through the foundation, which is continuous, but it is essential to provide expansion joints in the coping. In building work, movement joints must be sealed to prevent water penetration, to provide fire resistance and to maintain thermal insulation, but these factors do not affect landscape walls and therefore the need to seal open joints is a matter of appearance rather than compliance with building regulations. Sealants may be either gaskets in neoprene rubber or similar material which are built into the wall during construction, or soft mastics which are applied with a gun after the wall has been completed. Sealants of either type have to be flexible in order to take up movement without failure, and there are a very large number of them on the market whose composition is continually changing. Different bricks have different expansion and suction properties which affect the choice of sealant and the landscape designer is advised to consult the manufacturer about the most suitable sealant for a particular location. It is unlikely that sealant joints will be necessary in landscape walls, since neither privacy nor waterproofing are design requirements, and unless it is imperative to seal a movement joint it is better to leave them open and include them in the design. Some methods of forming movement joints are as follows:

- Simple straight breaks between two sections of wall. It looks better to leave a gap of 25 mm or so rather than the minimum space.

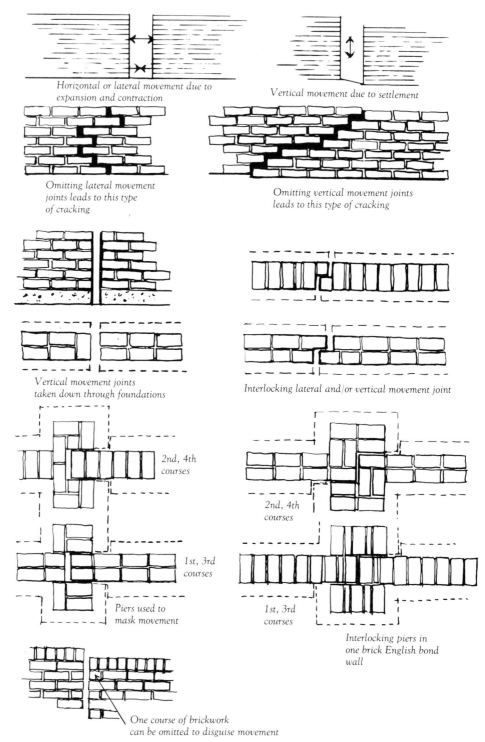

Horizontal or lateral movement due to expansion and contraction

Vertical movement due to settlement

Omitting lateral movement joints leads to this type of cracking

Omitting vertical movement joints leads to this type of cracking

Vertical movement joints taken down through foundations

Interlocking lateral and/or vertical movement joint

2nd, 4th courses

1st, 3rd courses

Piers used to mask movement

2nd, 4th courses

1st, 3rd courses

Interlocking piers in one brick English bond wall

One course of brickwork can be omitted to disguise movement

Figure 3.13   Movement joints

50

- Overlapping two sections of wall; this is only possible if the site allows for the extra space required.
- Interlocking the two sections, either with a half-and-half joint or with splayed joint. One-and-a-half-brick walls can accommodate a central nib and socket joint.
- Overlapping double-sided piers, so that one pier is attached to one section and the other pier is attached to the other section.

Vertical settlement joints

It is a fortunate landscape designer who is able to build all the landscape walls on firm undisturbed ground of equal consistency, and the vast majority of landscape walls will have to be built on variable and probably unstable ground. While it is possible to reinforce foundations to the extent that the walls are virtually carried on ground beams, it is preferable to allow for differential settlement by providing movement joints wherever there is a sharp distinction between two types of ground with different bearing capacities. This situation occurs where a landscape wall crosses an old road, a filled ditch, or made up levels, and even very low walls will be stressed by the change of ground. Where the wall crosses the line between one type and the other a vertical break should be provided both in the wall itself and in the foundations which will allow the two sections to slide vertically against each other if differential settlement takes place. If the design permits, it is sensible to combine expansion and settlement joints in order to reduce the number of breaks in the wall, and it is good practice to construct piers at these points, partly to strengthen the wall at a point of stress and partly to make a design feature of a constructional necessity.

3.6 ARCHES

There is nothing more attractive than the traditional well-designed brick arch forming the entrance to a walled garden. All qualified brickies are trained to construct arches as part of their normal curriculum, and there is therefore no reason why the landscape designer should not use these skills to create arches framing openings in brick or stone walls without incurring enormous expense. Arches are also very attractive when used in series to form arcades, either as a single arcade to frame a formal landscape or as a double arcade to enclose a formal walk, either open or with overhead beams. 'Blind' arcading is really an arcade built against the face of a backing wall, and can be used very charmingly to frame seating, carvings, maps or other objects in projects such as information centres, museums and similar buildings. It is extremely effective when placed around cloisters.

Plate 5   Arches   *A traditional arch in very thin bricks with stone jambs and springing. Because the bricks are very thin the joints appear to be parallel; with standard bricks the joints would be tapered, and either very thin at the intrados or very thick at the extrados. The alternative method of avoiding thick joints is to use radius bricks as voussoirs.*

Arch construction

The arch is a very old way of spanning openings and has developed a large and specialized vocabulary over the centuries. The terms most likely to be met by the landscape designer are as follows:

- The *springing*; the point from which the arch springs, or is supported by the wall below.
- *Springers* are the lowest bricks in the arch which starts from the springing.

Plate 6   Arches   *A small Roman arch in thin brick. The key brick has slipped slightly over the centuries, but the construction is nevertheless a neat and useful detail for small openings where wildlife, roots, or pipes must pass through a wall.*

- The *soffit* is the underside of the arch.
- The *intrados* and *extrados* are the inside and outside curves of the arch respectively.
- The *crown* is the highest point of the arch.
- The *abutment* is the brickwork which supports the arch.
- The *span* is the distance between the abutments.
- *Voussoirs* are the bricks or stones which form the arch.
- The *keystone* is the top brick or stone in the arch which in traditional construction locks the whole arch; it is often larger and stronger than the voussoirs. It is also traditionally used as a decorative feature carrying a coat of arms, a date, a symbol or a monogram.
- The *rise* is the distance between the springing and the intrados at the highest point of the arch.

Further terms will be found in the glossary.

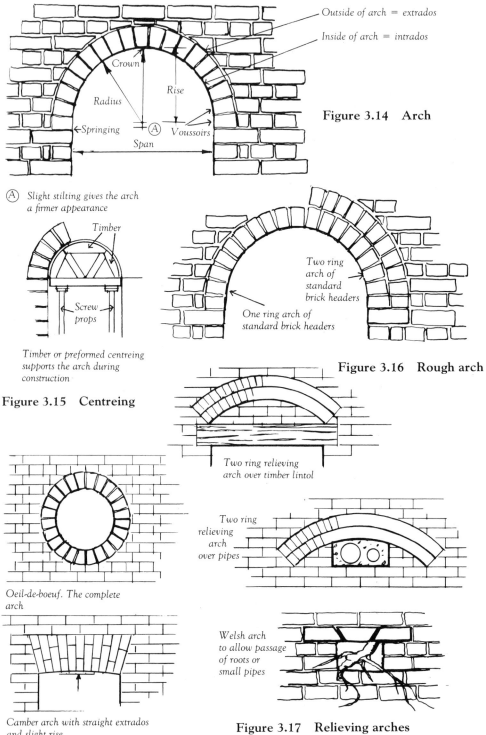

Outside of arch = extrados

Inside of arch = intrados

Crown

Rise

Radius

←Springing (A) Voussoirs

Span

Figure 3.14   Arch

(A)   Slight stilting gives the arch
a firmer appearance

Timber

Screw
props

Timber or preformed centreing
supports the arch during
construction

Figure 3.15   Centreing

Two ring
arch of
standard
brick headers

One ring arch of
standard brick headers

Figure 3.16   Rough arch

Two ring relieving
arch over timber lintol

Two ring
relieving
arch
over pipes

Oeil-de-boeuf. The complete
arch

Welsh arch
to allow passage
of roots or
small pipes

Camber arch with straight extrados
and slight rise

Figure 3.17   Relieving arches

54

Centreing

Although when built the arch is self-supporting and can carry very great loads evenly placed above it, some support is required while the arch is being constructed. Arches are traditionally built on centreing or turning pieces; these are rough timber frameworks on which the arch is built, and only removed after the mortar has completely set. To save time and cost, purpose-made arch formers in light steel are available for the most common forms and sizes of arch. Whatever type of centreing is used, the arch should not be loaded until the mortar has taken up its full set (See Figure 3.15).

Rough arches

The simplest and cheapest form of construction is the rough arch which is mostly used for garden work, and consists of one ring of bricks on end, or two rings of brick on edge. In rough arches the bricks are not cut or trimmed in any way. This means that the joints will be wider at the extrados than at the intrados and it is obvious that very small spans will have a coarse appearance which is acceptable for informal construction but not for fine work. Rough arches are best built in walls of rough rustic type facings where the irregularity of the joints is complemented by the irregularity of the bricks themselves (See Figure 3.16).

Axed arches

Ordinary bricks are used for these arches, where the bricks are cut to shape on site with a bolster or an angle grinder, giving shaped voussoirs with an even width joint of 10 mm. This looks much better on narrow spans than the rough arch but requires a lot of site work, and if the arch is anything other than a plain semicircle, each voussoir will have to be cut individually to a template which is an expensive operation. Hard burnt bricks which are liable to shatter when hit are obviously not suitable for axed work. BS 4729 on special bricks includes 'culvert' bricks which are virtually brick-on-edge voussoirs tapering from 75 mm to 55, 63 or 70 mm on the header face, and also brick-on-end voussoirs tapering from 75mm to 50, 55 or 63 mm on the stretcher face. Although not perfectly adapted to every arch profile, they are less expensive than cutting voussoirs on site and give a reasonable approximation to axed work, and they should be obtainable in most facings.

Gauged arches

These arches are not much used today except in restoration work. They are made of very soft bricks called rubbers which are ground to a very exact profile for each voussoir and can produce an arch with fine joints, often picked put in white cement mortar. If perfectly formed voussoirs are required for the design, it would be cheaper today to have voussoirs purpose-made or machine-cut by specialist firms.

Relieving arches

Rough arches placed in the solid wall to relieve the pressure of the wall on a stone or timber lintol are called relieving arches. They can also be built over a patch of soft ground, or over an underground service pipe or drain where pressure would be undesirable. Where the wall is constructed of large piers with a thin wall between them, upside-down relieving arches can be constructed to spring from the piers (with the extrados at the bottom) in order to distribute the pressure from the piers more evenly over the ground (See Figure 3.17).

Half-round arch

The simplest shape of arch is the half-round. This is a single-centred arch of the same diameter as the opening it surmounts. Assuming that people will pass through the arch, it is only suitable for openings up to 1000 mm, but beyond that span the rise – which is half the span – becomes too great for an opening in a landscape wall unless it is over 2400 mm high, since at least four courses of brickwork must be laid above the crown of the arch. These courses above the arch are required partly for appearance's sake, and partly because the voussoirs need to be weighted down for the arch to lock properly (See Figure 3.18).

Segmental arch

Where there is insufficient height over a half-round arch for the necessary brickwork, a segmental arch, which is a slice cut from a circle, may be used. It is not as strong as a half-round arch, nor does it look as attractive, but the height of the wall can be considerably less as the rise can be as little as one-sixth of the span. As the segment is usually derived from a large radius circle, standard or axed bricks may be used successfully instead of specials (See Figure 3.19).

Stilted arch

As its name suggests, this arch is a half-round arch set on 'stilts' which is the name for three or four courses of voussoirs laid horizontally like brick courses above the springing, so that the arch proper starts at a higher point than the true half-round arch. This form gives an impression of height to the opening but it can only be used in the walls 2700 mm or 3000 mm high if people are to pass through it. It can be a very attractive arch when used as an arcade framing a prospect, as the narrowing of the view combined with the arch form strengthens the effect of framing the view (See Figure 3.20).

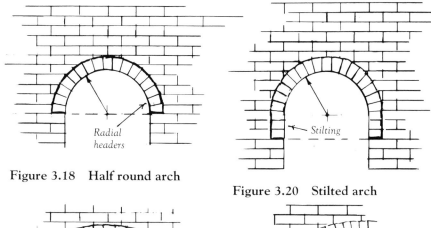

Radial
headers

Figure 3.18   Half round arch

Stilting

Figure 3.20   Stilted arch

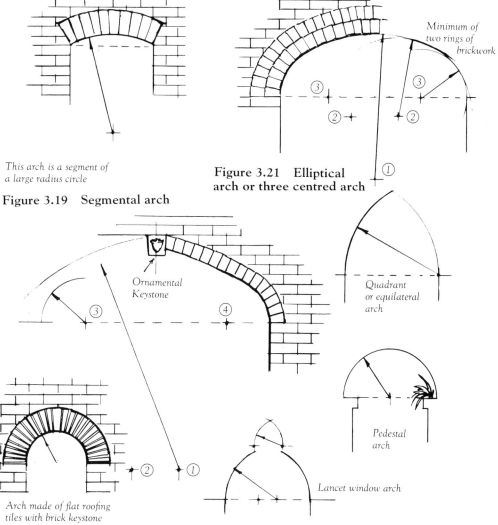

This arch is a segment of
a large radius circle

Figure 3.19   Segmental arch

Minimum of
two rings of
brickwork

**Figure 3.21   Elliptical
arch or three centred arch**

Ornamental
Keystone

Quadrant
or equilateral
arch

Pedestal
arch

Lancet window arch

Arch made of flat roofing
tiles with brick keystone

Figure 3.22   Four centred arch

Elliptical arch

These are best suited to rather low wide openings and were traditionally used for fireplace openings, though there are many opportunities to include these arches in landscape walls. The arch is not a true ellipse, since this would involve very complex cutting of the voussoirs, but is a three-centred arch giving a good approximation to an ellipse, and it looks best when the arch is composed of two or more rings of voussoirs, as a construction of one ring only emphasizes the variation from a true ellipse (See Figure 3.21).

Four-centred or Tudor arch

Similar to the elliptical arch in construction. It can be used successfully in the same positions, but the arch rises to a shallow point in the centre instead of following a smooth curve as in the elliptical arch. It is popularly associated almost exclusively with the vision of electric log fires, mock-Tudor beams and imitation horse brasses in pseudo-pubs, but none the less when properly constructed out of good bricks it is an elegant shape well suited to wide low openings in thick landscape walls. It should not be rejected because of its occasional misuse by bad designers (See Figure 3.22).

There are a number of other arch forms, such as Gothic, Moorish, or Dutch, but these are less likely to be used by the landscape designer, and the principles of setting out from two, three or four centres remain the same. The camber arch is really a lintol, and is described in the section on lintols.

3.7   LINTOLS

Lintols (or lintels; the spelling of building terms is variable) are plain beams of steel, timber or precast concrete used to carry brickwork over openings. They are much cheaper than arches and do not require so much wall height to accommodate them, but they can never create quite the same feeling of framing an opening that the arch gives. Properly built brickwork is cohesive, so that most of the weight of the wall above the lintol is distributed through the wall to each side of the opening. Thus, the actual weight carried by the lintol is not that of the full rectangular area of brickwork above it, but approximates to an equilateral triangle. It is structurally satisfactory to construct lintols from perforated brickwork reinforced with steel rods passed through the perforations, but because landscape walls are very exposed to weather, the risk of corrosion due to penetrating damp makes these lintols unreliable unless stainless steel rods are used. The intention is to make the bricks appear to span openings which they cannot naturally attain, but this may not be considered as good design, and it is probably preferable to express the lintol as a design feature.

Steel lintols

Steel is the strongest material for its weight, but it is very prone to rust after exposure to weather, and as it is unlikely that any commercial manager will include landscape walls in his maintenance schedule until they actually fall down, it is better not to use steel if it can be avoided. If it must be used, then it should be hot-dip galvanized and bedded in bitumen to prevent attack from the mortar. The usual type of steel lintol is the rolled steel angle, built with the longest flange vertical and with the bricks over the opening resting on the shorter flange. Only the edge of the flange is visible on the face of the wall; in a half-brick wall the flange will show on the back of the wall, but in a one brick wall where two angles are used back to back the flanges will be hidden in the central brick joint. A bearing of at least 150 mm should be provided in the wall on each side of the opening and the steel itself must rest on a padstone of precast concrete, Class A engineering brick, or natural stone. The most suitable steel-angle sizes for small openings up to 1000 mm wide are listed in Table 3.6. (See also Figure 2.23)

Table 3.6
Steel-angle lintols

half-brick wall	one 150 × 90 mm angle
	one 137 × 102 mm angle
one-brick wall	one 200 × 150 mm angle
one-brick wall	two 150 × 90 mm angles back to back
one-and-a-half-brick wall	two 200 × 150 mm angles back to back

There are a number of patent preformed steel lintols with various complex profiles used in the construction industry which allow facing bricks to be bedded on flanges projecting from the lintol, and the landscape designer who wishes to use steel lintols should examine the wide range available. Some of these lintols will span up to 4000 mm clear opening, but their appearance may not be satisfactory as they are mainly designed for concealed use in external building walls. Stainless steel, or hot-dip galvanizing together with epoxy resin coating is essential for external lintols. For large openings in excess of 1000mm a universal steel beam of I-section should be used if a plain lintol is required. These will take all normal landscape wall loads, but the maximum spans which should be allowed in order to avoid deflection are listed in Table 3.7.

Precast concrete lintols

Precast concrete lintols are more weatherproof and less prone to corrosion than steel lintols, but they are not very attractive as the finish is usually plain concrete as it comes from the mould. This may be improved by painting the lintol with cement paint, tooling the surface or etching the concrete with acid

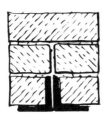
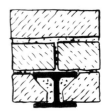

**Figure 3.23
Steel lintols**

*One ms angle
showing on back of
half brick wall*

*Two ms angles showing
under soffit of opening*

*Rolled steel beam
with cut bricks bedded on flanges*

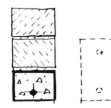

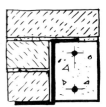

Precast lintols 65, 140, and 215mm high

Boot lintol

*Precast lintol
combined with
steel tray lintol*

Figure 3.24   Precast concrete lintols

*Light pressed steel tray lintols, not suitable
for severe
exposure*

*Hardwood
beams in pairs
with facing grain*

Figure 3.25   Timber lintols

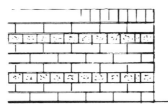

*String courses. Flush or slightly
projecting courses used to emphasize
horizontal effect*

Figure 3.26a   Ornamental brickwork

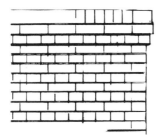

*Corbels. Used to support
wider coping or railing above,
or to give more massive
appearance to top of wall.*

Table 3.7
British Standard Beam lintols

for a span of 1500 mm use a 254 × 102 mm × 22 kg/m beam
or a 305 × 102 mm × 25 kg/m beam
for a span of 2000 mm use a 254 × 102 mm × 28 kg/m beam
or a 305 × 127 mm × 48 kg/m beam
or a 356 × 127 mm × 33 kg/m beam
for a span of 2500 mm use a 203 × 133 mm × 25 kg/m beam
or a 305 × 127 mm × 48 kg/m beam
or a 406 × 140 mm × 39 kg/m beam
or a 457 × 152 mm × 52 kg/m beam
for a span of 3000 mm use a 203 × 133 mm × 30 kg/m beam
or a 254 × 146 mm × 31 kg/m beam
or a 305 × 165 mm × 40 kg/m beam
or a 356 × 171 mm × 45 kg/m beam
or a 406 × 178 mm × 54 kg/m beam
or a 457 × 152 mm × 82 kg/m beam
or a 457 × 191 mm × 67 kg/m beam

to expose the aggregate, but they will always remain identifiable as concrete lintols. Concrete lintols are controlled by BS 5642: Parts 1 and 2, and if cast on site they should be made from C25 grade concrete or better and allowed to cure for five days minimum. Reinforcement for light lintols consists of four bars welded with cross-rods into a cage which is supplied ready-made from builder's merchants. Commercially available lintols are supplied 300 mm longer than the allowable clear span in order to provide a bearing of 150 mm on each side. The commonest sizes and spans are listed in Table 3.8.

In addition, there are precast concrete lintols intended for use in building work which have a concrete structural lintol combined with a galvanized and chemical-resistant paint-coated steel tray which carries the bricks on the face of the wall over the opening. The most useful type is designed for a one brick wall and consists of 100 mm concrete lintol 215 mm high with a 88 mm steel projecting tray. The tray may carry plain brick courses or brick-on-end facing. Permissible loads are shown in Table 3.9. (See also Figure 3.24).

Timber lintols

Timber lintols are not much used except for restoration and small-scale garden work, as there is a risk that the timber may rot unless it is properly maintained. This may be prevented either by using an expensive heavy hardwood such as jarrah, seasoned English oak, or greenheart, or by using softwood treated with preservative. The types of timber preservative are discussed in the section on fencing. Because it is not good practice to bolt two sections of timber together to make up the wall thickness, timber lintols are restricted in practice to half-brick-thick walls. The lintols must be set on

Table 3.8
Concrete lintols

Size	Clear Span	Safe distributed load in kN/m
215 × 100 mm	600 mm	15.0 k/Nm
	900	15.0
	1200	13.5
	1500	13.5
	1800	12.5
	2100	11.5
	2400	9.0
215 × 225 mm	900	15.0
	1200	15.0
	1500	13.5
	1800	13.5
	2100	12.5
	2400	11.5
	2700	9.0
150 × 200 mm	900	13.5
	1200	13.5
	1500	11.0
	1800	9.0
	2100	10.0

Table 3.9
Permissible loads

Clear Span	Safe distributed load in kN/m
600 mm	15.0 kN/m
900	15.0
1200	13.5
1500	13.5
1800	12.5
2100	12.5
2400	11.0
2700	9.0

Table 3.10
Timber lintols

100 mm wide × 100 mm high will span   600 mm
      × 150   900
      × 200   1000

padstones with a bearing of at least 150mm. Suitable sizes (also called scantlings) for timber lintols are shown in Table 3.10. (See also Figure 3.25).

3.8 ORNAMENTAL BRICKWORK

This form of decoration is being revived with the increasing use of bricks and the greater numbers of skilled brickies who have been trained in this art and who are now available. Brickwork decoration can be carried out to the landscape designer's drawings, but if the contractor is fortunate enough to employ a superb craftsman it is advisable to get his advice on the most suitable patterns, having regard to the type of brick chosen – landscape designers who require elaborate carving on hard engineering brick are popular neither with the brickie nor the client's accountant. The designs must be commensurate with the pocket of the client and with the level of craftsmanship available. For inspiration, the landscape designer could well look at the beautiful ornamental brickwork on the tall chimneys of some Tudor buildings – Oxenham in East Anglia is an outstanding example of ornamental brickwork. Most of the simple decorative brickwork described here should be carried out on walls at least one brick thick, and preferably one and a half bricks thick as the necessary variation of the bond may reduce the strength of the wall to some extent. Decoration may take a number of forms, many of which can be combined to create a magnificent effect. For example:

- Simple *string* courses. These are slightly projecting courses of bricks, either of the same shape as the main brickwork but of a different colour, or formed of one of the many special-shaped bricks such as plinth, bull-nosed, or splayed.
- *Lacing* courses. These are one, two or three courses of plain flat tiles built into the wall about 600 mm or 450 mm apart in order to give a strong horizontal emphasis. They should be bonded in a similar way to the bricks so that no continuous vertical joints are formed. (See figure 3.26b).
- *Plinths* are projecting courses of brickwork at the base of the wall. Besides giving the wall an appearance of great stability, they also serve the purpose of strengthening the base of an otherwise thin wall and protect the main face from scraping by traffic. They may project just a half-brick

63

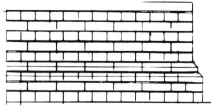

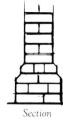

Section

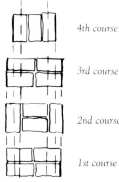

Wall

4th course

3rd course

2nd course

1st course

Plinths. Give an appearance of strength to the base of the wall and protect it from damage. Help to spread load on ground

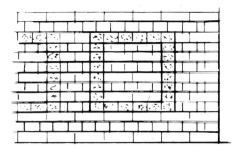

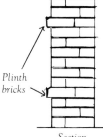

¾ bat

¾ bat

Plinth brick

Section

Coffering or panel work. Relieves long plain run of brickwork. Infill of panel can be in a different brick. The panel may be carved or used to display notices or artefacts.

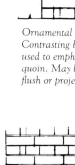

Plinth bricks

Section

Strap work. Slighly projecting bricks in different colour used to form letters or patterns

Ornamental quoins. Contrasting bricks used to emphasize quoin. May be flush or projecting

Perforated work. Alternative to honeycomb brickwork to provide views.

Section

Lacing course. Three courses of clay roofing tiles

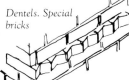

Dentels. Special bricks

Perforated work. Alternative to honeycomb brickwork to provide views.

Figure 3.26b   Ornamental brickwork

64

width, or be increased at each course to give a width at the base of the wall much greater than the wall itself (See Figure 3.26b).

- *Corbels* are projecting courses at the top of the wall, usually just under the coping, which overhang the lower part and give a strong finish to the skyline. They can be used very successfully to widen a dwarf wall to make it usable as a seat whilst leaving foot space underneath (See Figure 3.26a).
- *Strap-work* is the name for lozenges, squares, circles (rather difficult), lettering or logos picked out on the face of the wall by projecting bricks of a strongly contrasting colour (See Figure 26b and Plate 7).
- *Diaper-work* is the use of contrasting headers in an ordinary bond but arranged to form diamonds, squares, vertical or diagonal lines.
- *Pierced-work* is brickwork with a series of openings formed in it which may be larger or smaller than the solid brickwork between the openings. It is mostly used for ornamental balustrading, and can be very attractive if it frames planting or landscape vistas, but the landscape designer must take care that the balustrade is safe for both adults and children.
- *Coffering* is the construction of recessed panels in the wall, giving a modelling which is especially attractive where the angle of the light can emphasize the coffering. It is essential to use plinth bricks for the lower edge of the coffer, as if plain bricks are used there will be a water-retaining ledge where frost can attack the brick work (See Figure 3.26b).
- *Herring-bone* brickwork, where the bricks are set at 45°, is a traditional form of decorative brickwork, but it has little strength and must only be used in panels framed by structural brickwork.

3.9   REINFORCED BRICK WALLS

The calculation of fully reinforced structural brick walls is a matter for the structural engineer, but simple reinforcement, designed to prevent slight subsidence movement or to strengthen the wall against pressure on the face, can be included in the landscape specification. There are two main types of reinforcement; stainless steel expanded mesh such as Exmet which is easy to bend up and down and can be folded round corners to accommodate changes in direction; and welded 3 mm steel wire mesh such as Brickforce which consists of two or three parallel wires connected by lateral wires at about 400 mm centres. These reinforcing materials should be built into the wall every three courses and lapped at least 75 mm at joints. Expanded steel mesh is made slightly narrower than the brickwork so that there is no danger of the steel becoming exposed, and it is available for 105, 215 and 330 mm wall thicknesses. As well as reinforcing walls, it is very useful as a means of strengthening piers when they are liable to settlement or impact stresses. Welded stainless steel mesh reinforcement helps the wall to resist lateral

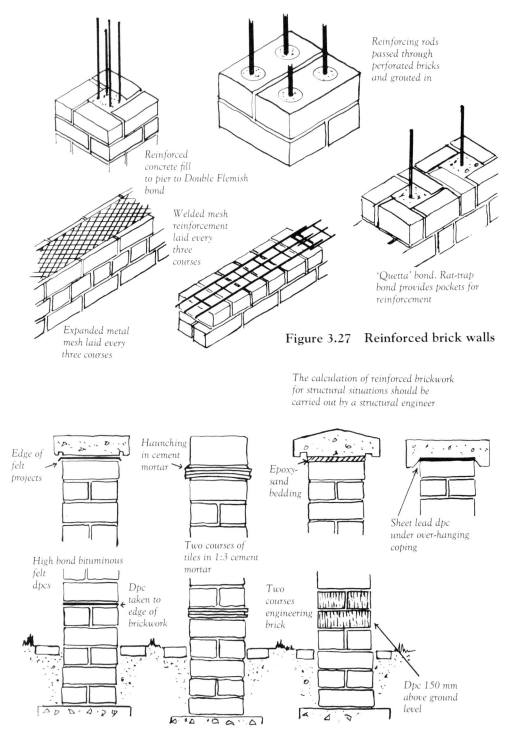

Reinforcing rods passed through perforated bricks and grouted in

Reinforced concrete fill to pier to Double Flemish bond

Welded mesh reinforcement laid every three courses

Expanded metal mesh laid every three courses

'Quetta' bond. Rat-trap bond provides pockets for reinforcement

Figure 3.27 Reinforced brick walls

The calculation of reinforced brickwork for structural situations should be carried out by a structural engineer

Edge of felt projects

Haunching in cement mortar

Epoxy-sand bedding

Sheet lead dpc under over-hanging coping

High bond bituminous felt dpcs

Dpc taken to edge of brickwork

Two courses of tiles in 1:3 cement mortar

Two courses engineering brick

Dpc 150 mm above ground level

Figure 3.28 Dampproof courses

66

Plate 7   Ornamental brickwork   *Crystal Palace Park identified in dark blue engineering brick set in pale buff clay bricks. The pattern is formed of standard stretchers and headers uncut, and laid flush with the wall surface, providing a vandal proof and permanent decoration. Cut bricks would have given a more refined pattern, but the detail shown is comparatively cheap and simple to construct. A pier designed with contrasting brick patterns is shown in plate 28.*

pressure and settlement and it is also useful to provide additional stiffening of the wall over openings. It is manufactured in 40, 60, 100 and 160 mm widths (See Figure 3.27).

Perforated bricks

Perforated bricks are used in walls to allow vertical steel reinforcing rods to be passed down through the wall in order to stiffen it against lateral pressure, somewhat on the lines of a retaining wall. This method is suitable for lightly loaded walls such as those carrying overhead beams for pergolas which may have a lateral thrust, or even for dwarf walls retaining earth up to 500 mm high, but they are no substitute for a properly designed retaining wall. It is difficult to ensure that the rods are overlapped at vertical joints, and almost

Plate 8   Ornamental brickwork   *Panels of bricks set cornerways in a plain brickwork surround. This ornamentation gives a rich texture to the otherwise rather dull one brick wall, though as it is weaker than ordinary bonds, it should not be used where strength is important. A single or double row of angled bricks are called dentils. Birdsmouth bricks are available which give a similar effect, but which enable the bricks to be laid in an ordinary bond.*

impossible to see that the contractor fills all the perforations with mortar; while it is a heartbreaking job for the brickie to thread each brick over a rod and slide it down to rest on exactly the right amount of mortar bed.

3.10   DAMP-PROOF COURSES (DPCs)

There are two places where damp proof courses are required in a landscape wall: the wall DPC placed just above ground level and the coping DPC placed immediately under the coping. All DPCs must be the full thickness of the wall and should finish flush with the wall face; if any mortar is allowed to bridge the DPC then the water will travel across the DPC and make it useless (See Figure 3.28).

Wall DPCs

The wall damp-proof course should be placed not less than 150 mm above the ground level; its purpose is to prevent damp and the consequent algal disfiguration, and to prevent deleterious ground salts from travelling up the wall by osmosis. After construction, earth is often piled against the wall above the DPC by gardeners and it is a frequent cause of wall deterioration. Water which has travelled up the wall from the ground and then frozen may also cause the exposed brick face to spall if the bricks are absorbent. There are several materials suitable for landscape wall DPCs: engineering brick, slate, bituminous d.p.c.s., or expoxy-sand.

Two courses of engineering brick (or any other brick which has a maximum water absorption of 4.5 per cent for wet areas, or 7 per cent for dryer areas) are required laid in 1:3 cement:sand mortar, though if the bricks of the wall itself have a low moisture absorption and the site is continuously dry then the DPC may be omitted. For retaining walls, or any wall where there is an imposed load on the face of the wall, engineering brick must be used as there is then no risk of the wall slipping over the DPC.

Two courses of slates may be laid lapped in the same mortar mix (the traditional specification for a slate DPC reads 'lay two courses of undressed ladies on an even bed'. Ladies were a particular size of slate and undressed means that the slates were not holed as they would be for roofing; the bed was mortar). Slates being rather brittle, the mortar bed must be laid very evenly and the slates firmly bedded; they should not be used where there is a risk of vertical settlement.

Bituminous DPCs must be to BS 6398; Class D hessian base and lead, Class E fibre base and lead, or Class F asbestos base and lead and lapped at least 150 mm at joints. Lead alone is likely to extrude under pressure and to discolour brickwork.

Epoxy resin and sand mixture 6 mm thick makes a good DPC for angles, curves, and piers, as it can be laid to the shape of the wall. At least 15 per cent resin should be used, and careful site supervision is essential. (See Figure 3.28)

Coping DPCs

The function of the coping DPC is to prevent water travelling down the wall, causing staining and possibly frost spalling of the brick face. These DPCs may be made of the following materials:

- High-bond bituminous felt as described above; types D and E; ordinary bitfelt is less adhesive and is likely to allow the coping to be pushed off.
- Lead is permissible where the coping clasps the top of the wall so that it cannot be moved, but it must be coated with bituminous paint to prevent interaction with the bricks.
- Engineering brick copings bedded in 1:3 cement:sand mortar are sufficiently water resistant in themselves to allow the DPC to be omitted.

69

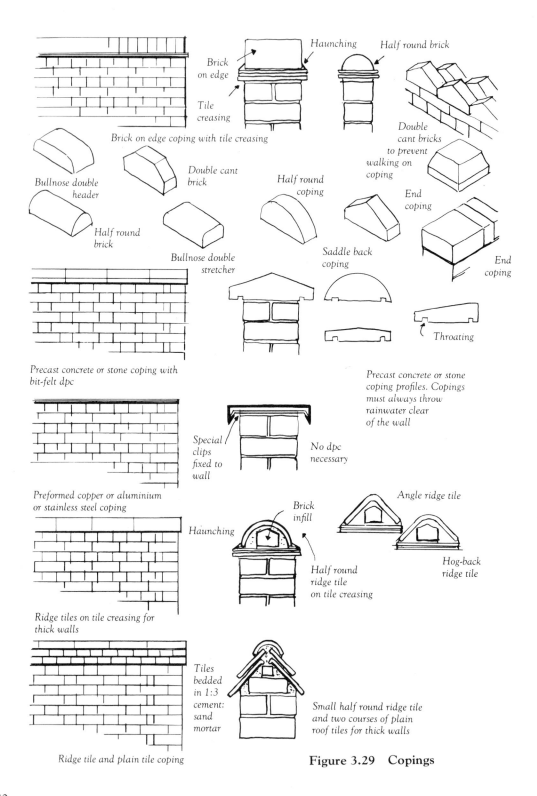

Brick on edge

Haunching

Half round brick

Tile creasing

Brick on edge coping with tile creasing

Double cant bricks to prevent walking on coping

Bullnose double header

Double cant brick

Half round coping

End coping

Half round brick

Bullnose double stretcher

Saddle back coping

End coping

Throating

Precast concrete or stone coping with bit-felt dpc

Special clips fixed to wall

No dpc necessary

Precast concrete or stone coping profiles. Copings must always throw rainwater clear of the wall

Preformed copper or aluminium or stainless steel coping

Haunching

Brick infill

Angle ridge tile

Half round ridge tile on tile creasing

Hog-back ridge tile

Ridge tiles on tile creasing for thick walls

Tiles bedded in 1:3 cement: sand mortar

Small half round ridge tile and two courses of plain roof tiles for thick walls

Ridge tile and plain tile coping

Figure 3.29   Copings

- Pre-formed copper, aluminium or stainless steel copings are completely waterproof if properly joined at the laps. These are most likely to be used where landscape walls are part of a high-tech design based on metal structures.
- Two courses of well-burnt clay tiles lapped and tilted slightly towards the face of the wall are satisfactory, but the tiles must be water resistant in themselves and bedded in 1:3 cement:sand mortar.

3.11   COPINGS

The wall coping should be in keeping with the character and function of the wall itself; for example, a light brick-on-edge coping would be suitable for a low half-brick or one-brick boundary wall, a heavy flat stone or concrete coping where the wall is to be used as a seat, or a steeply pitched concrete coping where children must not run along the wall. (See Figure 3.29). All copings, whatever they are made of, must perform three functions:

- Overhang the wall by at least 35 mm on each side in order to throw the rain well clear of the wall face.
- Provide a waterproof and frostproof capping to the wall to prevent water seeping down through the brickwork.
- Have a 'throating' or groove on the underside of the overhang at least 10 mm wide and 5 mm deep in order to prevent water running back under the overhang and so down the wall.

Brick-on-edge

This is composed of bricks on edge with a plain tile 'creasing' (two courses of well-burnt clay tiles laid lapped). The tile creasing is traditional in most areas of England and it gives a strong visual finish to the wall but it is liable to chipping by people or vehicles on walls below shoulder height. It is usual to use the same bricks as those in the wall itself, but a harder brick or an engineering brick may be used where strength or high water resistance is required or a darker brick can be used to emphasize the top of the wall. Good roofing tiles are made with a slight camber to shed rain and they should be laid so that this camber falls towards the outside of the wall. The tiles are bedded in 1:3 cement:sand mortar and should be lapped at least one-third of their width. Roofing tiles have two nibs for fixing to the tiling batten and these nibs may be removed (carefully) by the brickie when they are laid, or left facing outward to form a decorative feature. Flat concrete roofing tiles can be used, but the visual effect is poor and they are less water resistant. Brick-on-edge coping at the end of a wall is often finished off with a cramp iron bedded under the last three or four courses of coping bricks and turned up to restrain the end brick. This is not a recommended practice as when the

Plate 9   Brick on edge coping   *Brick on edge coping with tile creasing. The tiles are properly slanted to throw off rain, and lapped to prevent water travelling down the wall.*

angle iron has rusted away the end bricks fall off and the wall is then easily damaged. It is preferable to finish the wall with a pier which has a properly bonded brick coping or to use a special brick coping block to match the wall; these are now produced by most brickmakers.

Purpose-made brick copings

Purpose-made brick copings are manufactured to tone with most facing bricks. They can have many different profiles; flat, half round, sloping and other profiles are available either as standard or as specials made to order from brick manufacturers, and corner units for external and internal angles are manufactured. They are sometimes available to match a particular brick rather than to match a range of facing bricks, though matching copings for handmade facings would probably have to be ordered specially and are too expensive to be used for any but prestige contracts. They are bedded on 1:3 cement: sand mortar and should be laid on a non-slip DPC unless the wall is very sheltered.

Pre-cast stone or concrete copings

Purpose made precast stone or concrete copings are covered by BS 5642: Part 2:1983. It is not practicable to cast them on site as it is very difficult to get consistent colour and texture by this method. Commercially available copings are available in a wide range of profiles, colours and textures and they should be bedded in the same way as purpose made brick copings. Some types are made with waterproof interlocking joints which obviate the need for a DPC underneath.

Metal copings

Also available, but little used in landscape work are the preformed sheet metal copings; copper, aluminium, or stainless steel are the most common types. These are flat or slightly sloped profiles and are manufactured in long lengths. Though they give a 'cut-off' appearance to the top of the wall they are useful where water penetration is a problem and brick or stone copings would be liable to damage. Copper may stain the wall below if acid rainwater is allowed to run over the DPC, so that the coping above must project well over the DPC. Aluminium may break down in a corrosive atmosphere unless it is given a protective PVF2 powder coating. Preformed aluminium alloy copings are clipped on to the top of the wall with special clips screwed to the wall. Sections are waterproofed at the joints with neoprene seals. The coping is supplied self-colour or factory coated, and gives a clean mechanical finish to the wall that is in keeping with associated high-tech buildings. Aluminium copings are made in lengths of 3000 mm and standard widths are 182 and 212mm for half-brick walls, 272 and 302 for one-brick walls and specials can be made for thicker walls. Tee-junctions, corners and end-pieces are available.

Special bricks

Standard special bricks make good wall copings as they are usually available to match the facing brick and give a consistent appearance to the wall. Most of the standard special bricks can be used as brick-on-edge; these include single bull-nose, double bull-nose, double bull-nose stop end in pairs, bull-nose double header on flat, single cant, double cant, plinth header, and king closer. Most of the special coping bricks and precast stone or concrete

Plate 10   Precast concrete coping   *A rather thin precast concrete coping laid on two courses of corbels with a course of special brick dentils below it. The workmanship does no credit to the design, and the landscape designer must match the design to the quality of craftsmanship available; if special skills are required this must be specified in the contract.*

copings have matching end-blocks with the pattern returning so that the end of the wall can be neatly completed. These bricks are laid on a tile creasing in the same way as ordinary brick-on-edge, since they are not wide enough to provide an overhang by themselves. Where the landscape wall is high, wide and handsome, a compound coping may be designed using special bricks in two or three courses, possibly crowned with a hog-back or half-round ridge tile, but the coping must always be designed to suit the scale of the wall.

74

Ridge tiles

In some parts of the country half-round or saddle-back ridge tiles bedded on a tile creasing are traditional; they give a bulky effect and are not suitable for small walls or half-brick walls, but can be effective on large one-brick walls and are useful where people must be prevented from walking on the wall.

Tile capping

Very thick walls of two-brick thickness or over were often protected by constructing a narrow tiled roof over them. Two courses of plain clay tiles, laid and lapped as they would be on a roof, with a pitch of 40° or 45°, were bedded in lime mortar on a brick core raised above the top of the wall and finished with a narrow ridge tile bedded on top. Alternatively, the tiles may be laid sloping from one side of the wall to the other at a pitch of 35° or 30° and overhanging both sides of the wall, when a ridge tile will not be necessary. This type of coping is associated more with Spanish-style walls to courtyards, but it is a good sound weatherproof detail and gives big thick walls a coping which is in proportion to the scale of the wall.

3.12   MORTARS FOR WALLS

The choice of mortar for landscape walls is almost as important as the choice of brick, since the colour, texture and shape of the mortar joint can make a great deal of difference to the look of the wall. Site-mixed mortars are not specified in any British Standards, but BS 4721:1981 covers ready-mixed mortars. Bricklaying mortar is composed of sand, cement, lime, pigments, and various additives which change the character of the mortar, making it more frost-resistant, easier to handle, or slower to set.

Sand

The sand for bricklaying is controlled by BS 1199 and 1200:1976. Sand for bricklaying is quite different from that used for plastering and the two types should not be interchanged. Sand must be clean well-washed pit or river sand, free from all extraneous matter. In conditions of severe exposure, the sand must be rather coarser than usual and a sand of grade M in BS 882 will be satisfactory. The colour of the sand naturally affects the final colour of the mortar, so that it is important to ensure that all the sand for the job comes from the same source and preferably delivered in one batch. Sand colour ranges from nearly white through yellow, buff or grey to russet; if the wall is a conspicuous part of the design it may be worth instructing the contractor to prepare sample panels of brickwork with different coloured and profiled joints in order to choose the best combination which enhances the brick-work. The preparation of sample panels is an ordinary part of a building contract and the landscape designer may be able to take advantage of panels

Plate 11   Ridge tile   *A bold and effective detail. Although traditionally used for two or three brick thick walls, the coping here is supported on two corbel courses with dentils below. A wide coping like this provides some protection against frost for wall fruit and delicate climbers.*

prepared for the main building work; if not, a small sum to cover this work should be included in the contract.

Cement

The cement is usually Portland cement to BS 12:1989 and is used for all normal above ground work. Below ground ordinary Portland cement may be used unless sulphate attack is likely, in which case sulphate-resisting Portland cement to BS 4027:1980 should be used; when there is inadequate information about ground conditions it is better to specify sulphate-resisting cement rather than to risk sulphate attack. Masonry cement to BS 5224:1976 is much used for brickwork; it consists of ordinary Portland cement, a neutral filling material and an air entraining additive to which are added sand and water but never lime. Masonry cement is easier to work than the ordinary cement:lime mixtures and more frost resistant, but it is not so strong and its main advantage is speed and ease of use; it should not be used where the wall is subject to heavy loading or for retaining walls.

Lime

Lime is covered by BS 890:1972, and either ready-prepared lime putty, or hydrated lime powder may be used on site, being mixed with sand and left for at least 16 hours before use. Traditionally, fresh quicklime was used which was 'slaked' with water on site to form lime putty. The heat given off by this process was considerable, and particles of flying lime could cause eye injury and skin burns, so that this method is no longer used. It is now common practice to buy ready-mixed lime and sand to BS 4721, to which cement and water are added on site. If a coloured mortar is required the pigment is usually added to the lime–sand mix at the factory to ensure consistent colouring.

Additives

There are a number of additives which affect the workability or durability of mortars, and the most useful ones are plasticizers, accelerators, and retarders. Plasticicizers are usually based on polymerized resins, and they are added to increase the 'butteriness' of the mortar; they also increase the frost resistance of the mortar during bricklaying or pointing. It is well known in the trade that an equally easy-to-work mix may be obtained by the addition of small quantities of ordinary household detergent. This practice should never be permitted and the presence of empty detergent bottles on site demands investigation, since building workers are not given to extensive washing up. Accelerators are used, mainly in concrete work, to hasten the setting time of the work so that the next stage can proceed, but in landscape work there should not be any need for early strength in freestanding walls, and their use in retaining walls should only be allowed in special cases and then under close supervision. Retarders extend the working time of mortar mixes, and are mostly used in ready-mixed mortars delivered in bulk, since they allow the mortar to stay usable much longer than usual. Standard cement:lime:sand factory-mixed mortar is a retarded 1:1:6 mix capable of staying open for 36 hours, and standard cement:sand factory-mix mortar is a retarded 1:3 mix suitable for below ground and retaining wall work. Admixtures also include colours for mortar, and it is advisable to get all the mortar for one wall from a single batch of site-mix or ready-mix if possible, since even under factory conditions it is difficult to ensure perfect matching of batches. Ready-mixed mortars are also available as dry mixes of sand and lime which have the cement added on site as described above, and the advantage of these is that fresh cement may be added as required and in varying proportions.

There are a number of other additives such as epoxy resins, polyester resins and styrene butadiene rubber which increase the adhesive properties of the mortar, but these should not be needed in landscape wall construction except in very exceptional circumstances, when the manufacturer's advice should be sought.

Coloured mortars

The colour of the mortar may be selected to contrast with the brick if it is desired to emphasize the individual bricks, or selected to match the brick so that the wall has a homogeneous appearance. When possible, it is better to choose a naturally coloured sand to get the required colour, since even the best artificial pigments supplied by reputable firms have a way of looking shabby after some years. Ordinary Portland cement is grey, which affects the mortar colour, and it may be necessary to specify the more expensive white Portland cement if a very light mortar is wanted. When joints are struck flush, the coloured mortar will have to be used throughout, but if the wall is to be pointed, then plain mortar may be used for the construction, and the more expensive coloured mortar reserved for the pointing, though the mix must remain constant. Mortar may be had in pretty well any colour: white, grey, yellow, purple, red, black, brown, or any shade in between and from very dark to almost white, though the proportion of pigment should not exceed 10 per cent of the cement by weight. Mixing colours on site is not satisfactory, and ready-mixed mortars of any colour can always be supplied by a specialist firm.

Mortar mixes

BS 5628: Part 3: 1985 gives a series of recommended mortars for brick and blockwork; the proportions given are measured by volume since aggregates may vary considerably in weight according to their source. Those most often used in landscape work are listed in Table 3.11. The lower proportion of sand given in the mixes is for sand grade G in BS 1200, while the higher proportion is for sand grade S in BS 1200. The group of mortar specified will vary according to the location, the type of brick, and in the case of brickwork below ground, the soil conditions (See Table 3.12). Sulphate resisting cement (OPSRC) should be used where there is a risk of sulphate attack either below ground or from high-salt-content bricks. If the wall has a full coping which throws the rain well clear of the wall OPC may be used, but if the wall has a flush capping only, then OPSRC should be used.

Table 3.11
Mortar mixes

Type of mix	Group 1	Group 2	Group 3	Group 4
cement:lime:sand	1: ¼:3	1: ½: 4 or 1: ½: 4 ½	1: 1: 5 or 1: 1: 6	1: 2: 8 or 1: 2: 9
cement: pre-mixed lime:sand	1:3	1: 4 or 1: 4 ½	1: 5 or 1: 6	1: 8 or 1: 9
(pre mixed lime:sand)	(1: 12)	(1: 9)	(1: 6)	(1: 4 ½)
masonry cement:sand	N/A	1:2 ½ or 1: 3 ½	1: 4 or 1: 5	1: 5 ½ or 1: 6 ½

Table 3.12
Use of mortars

Location	Clay brick	Calcium silicate brick	Concrete brick
brickwork below ground in dry conditions	Group 3	Group 3	Group 3
brickwork below ground in wet conditions	Group 2	Group 3	Group 3
brick DPCs	Group 1	N/A	N/A
landscape walls in exposed situations	Group 2	Group 3	Group 3
landscape walls in sheltered situations	Group 3	Group 3	Group 3
rendered landscape walls	Group 3	Group 3	Group 3
copings to walls	Group 1	Group 2	Group 2
plinths, string courses and other projections	Group 1	Group 2	Group 2

3.13   BRICKWORK JOINTS

The shape of the joint has an equally critical effect on the appearance of the wall. Traditionally, elaborate-shaped joints were used on high-class work, sometimes using two different coloured mortars, but it would be difficult to find a brickie today who could do such work, and the cost would be considerable. The style of the joint must also suit the brick; rough-textured facings look best with flush-struck joints, while smooth hard arrised bricks look best with a sharply weathered joint. Joints may be formed as the work proceeds,

Rough hand made bricks
with wide flush joints

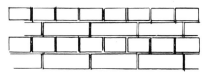

Sharp arrised engineering bricks
with narrow struck joints

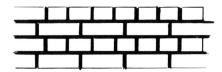

Light coloured bricks with dark
mortar joints emphasizes the joints

Dark coloured bricks with
light joints makes brickwork
look monolithic

Flush struck
joint as the work
proceeds

Recessed
joint pressed in
with tool

Bucket handle
joint

Hosepipe
joint

Flush joint
jointed

Weather struck

Mason's joint

Weather struck
and cut

Pointing. Joint
raked out 16 mm
and pointed

Figure 3.30   Joints in brickwork

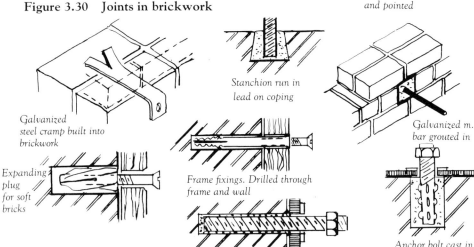

Galvanized
steel cramp built into
brickwork

Stanchion run in
lead on coping

Galvanized m.s.
bar grouted in

Expanding
plug
for soft
bricks

Frame fixings. Drilled through
frame and wall

Chemical bond bolt in pre-drilled hole

Anchor bolt cast in
concrete pocket

Figure 3.31   Fixings to brickwork

which makes for a stronger wall, or the joints may be left open to a maximum depth of 15 mm and pointed after completion, which makes for a neater joint. Pointing after completion of the main wall has the advantage that the work is likely to be carried out by the same brickie and with the same batch of mortar, which is particularly important if coloured mortar is being used. The mortar for pointing should be of the same strength as that used for the wall construction. No joint should be used which leaves a horizontal ledge to trap rain (See Figure 3.30). The commonest joints are as follows:

- *Flush struck*: the mortar is struck off flush with the face of the work with the trowel as the work proceeds.
- *Flush and dragged*: the joint is struck flush and a piece of coarse sacking (nowadays a woven polythene potato sack) is dragged along the joint while the mortar is still workable.
- *Recessed*: the joint is set back from the face by pressing with a round or oval-shaped tool – not a square one, as a square recess leaves a ledge to collect water which freezes and damages the wall. Both this joint and other pressed joints have the advantage that the mortar is pressed into close contact with the bricks so that there is no gap where water can lodge and freeze.
- *Bucket-handle*: recessed but with a slight moulding.
- *Pipe*: some hosepipes have a ridged surface which makes a pleasant slightly textured recessed joint. Brickies often make or adapt their own gadgets to produce individual styles of joint.
- *Flush joint jointed*: a narrow recess is formed in the centre of the joint which emphasizes the line and also compresses the mortar into the joint. This needs to be done very neatly if it is to look satisfactory, but when well done it is a smart joint suitable for hard arrised precise brickwork.
- *Weather struck*: the trowel is run along the joint at an angle, thus undercutting the top course and finishing flush with the lower course. The perpends are weathered on both sides to give a central ridge. This joint gives a strong horizontal emphasis, as the upper course casts a shadow. The striking should not be more than a 45° angle. The joint should never be struck the opposite way round, that is, with the lower course recessed, as this is a certain way to cause frost damage.
- *Struck and cut*: struck from top and bottom of the joint to give a 'V' profile.
- *Mason's joint*: a slightly projecting ridged joint with top and bottom faces bevelled, traditionally used for stonework.
- *Tuck pointing* (or bastard tuck pointing): a method of forming a false joint in weathered brickwork by filling the old widened joint with mortar to match the brickwork and then forming a new joint with contrasting mortar. It is not satisfactory in landscape walls as the joint eventually exposes its falsity and the brickwork looks worse than ever.

Table 3.13
Render mixes

Type of mix	Group 1	Group 2	Group 3	Group 4
cement:lime:sand	1:¼:3	1:½:4 or 1:½:4 ½	1:1:5 or 1:1:6	1:2:8 or 1:2:9
cement: pre-mixed lime:sand	1:3	1:4 or 1:4 ½	1:5 or 1:6	1: 8 or 1:9
(pre-mix lime:sand)	(1:12)	(1:9)	(1:6)	(1:4 ½)
plasticized cement:sand	N/A	1:3 or 1:4	1:5 or 1:6	1: 7 or 1:8
masonry cement:sand	N/A	1:2 ½ or 1:3 ½	1:4 or 1:5	1:5 ½ or 1:6 ½

3.14   RENDERING

Rendering is the term used for applying one or more coatings of cement:sand or cement:lime:sand mix to the face of the wall. The practice of rendering is covered in BS 5492:1977. It is used to cover up old damaged walls, to provide a very light reflective finish or to make the wall face impervious to water or chemicals, while some types of rendering are an attractive finish in themselves. Those most likely to be used in landscape work are plain cement: lime:sand render, 'harling' or rough-cast, plaster-work (this does not imply plaster as we know it today) and pebble-dash. In addition to these traditional finishes there are many proprietary renders on the market which are applied by specialist sub-contractors and which have a distinctive character. Rendering has to strike a balance between a strong mix which is weatherproof and vandal resistant and which will cause a weak brick backing to spall off; and a weak mix which is easily damaged and not impervious to moisture. The four main standard mixes are shown in Table 3.13. Very soft crumbly brickwork needs special treatment before rendering and calcium silicate bricks may need a bonding agent applied to their surface to provide an adequate key. Engineering bricks cannot be rendered successfully without special preparation. The mixes suitable for rendering of normal brickwork are shown in Table 3.14.

Plain render

Rendering must be provided with a suitable backing if it is to remain firmly attached to the wall; rough clay bricks, and some calcium silicate and concrete bricks may be sufficiently rough to provide adhesion, but smooth dense brickwork should have the joints raked out or left open during building in order to give a key; alternatively a bonding agent may be used. If mortar joints in existing walls are very hard the wall may be picked or roughened to

Table 3.14
Use of render mixes

Background	Undercoat	Finishing coat
Dense clay brick:		
plain render	mix 2	mix 3
roughcast	mix 2	mix 2
pebble dash	mix 2	mix 2
Normal clay brick:		
plain render	mix 3	mix 4
roughcast	mix 2	mix 2
pebble dash	mix 2	mix 2

give a key. Dense brickwork should be kept dry before rendering, but more absorbent surfaces should be dampened slightly to prevent the water in the rendering from being sucked out before the render has time to set; though excessive water may cause efflorescence to develop. Should the backing be very absorbent, or if rendering has to be carried out in hot dry weather, a water-retaining additive may be included in the mix to prevent premature drying-out. Two coats are usually applied but over very uneven surfaces three coats may be needed to give a smooth finish. There may be one or more undercoats needed to bring the background to a level surface, but the minimum thickness is 10 mm or 15 mm in very exposed conditions; these are composed of one of the mixes given above, which is scored lightly before it sets to provide a key for the final coat. The final coat, selected from the standard mixes above, should be as thin as is practicable to prevent cracking, with an average thickness of 6 mm. It may be given a textured surface in several different ways: by a wood float which gives a smooth but softly textured surface; by scraping or combing the half-set surface with a tool to give various markings; by working patterns in the render with a trowel; or even impressing patterns with the hand or shaped wooden stamps.

Harling or rough-cast

Harling in Scotland; rough-cast in England. Instead of the smooth final coat of plain render, 5 mm to 15 mm gravel or broken stone aggregate is mixed with a soft render selected from the table above and thrown onto the wall so that it adheres and forms a soft-textured finish which produces very attractive shadows from adjoining planting. It is usually white, cream, pale yellow or pale buff in colour and if a pure white is required it will be necessary to use white Portland cement. Harling is a skilled trade and the landscape designer should make sure that such labour is available before specifying this finish.

Pebble-dash or Dry-dash

This is usually associated with 1930s housing estates, but the fact that it is still in good condition on these houses shows that it is a very hard-wearing, graffiti-proof and self-cleaning finish which can be used in dirty atmospheres where lighter finishes would soon look shabby. It is created by throwing selected angular plain or coloured gravel – Thames gravel is suitable – onto a soft render so that the gravel embeds itself in this backing, leaving about one-half of the gravel surface showing above the render. It is not every workman who can do good pebble-dash and specialist firms should be nominated to do the work.

3.15 FIXINGS TO BRICKWORK

If the landscape designer intends to fix trellises, notices, handrails, guardrails, or any other object to the wall, then the fixings should be built into the wall or properly inserted with bolts when the wall has had time to harden, since a powerful hammer drill with a large labourer behind it can cause considerable damage to a newly built wall. The screws or bolts used for fixing items to walls are usually driven into a plug or special socket pushed into a hole drilled in the wall, and the strength of the fixing is dependent on the friction between the expanded socket and the brickwork. It is essential that the holes are drilled to the correct size for the bolt or screw to be used, as too large a hole allows the bolt to pull out under strain, and too small a hole may cause the bolt to split the brickwork when it is driven home. All screws or bolts should be stainless steel, brass, bronze, or other non-corrodible metal, since the expansion caused by corrosion will either split the brickwork or loosen the fixing or both. For light items such as notices or indicators, small plugs and screws up to 4 mm will be adequate, but where fixings such as handrails which serve to prevent accidents are to be fixed a much stronger fixing is necessary. These are steel, stainless steel or other non-corrodible metal threaded sockets into which 6, 8, 10 or 12 mm bolts, studs, threaded eye-bolts, rings or hooks may be set. The manufacturer of the item to be fixed will give guidance on the size and strength of fixing required. If possible, holes should be drilled in the bricks themselves and not in the joints, and no hole should be nearer than 150 mm from any edge of brickwork. Some manufacturers make chemical sockets in which the bolt breaks a small vial of chemical which forms a bond between the brickwork and the bolt, but these cannot be removed after fixing, so that only studs with removable nuts should be used to fix items if this type of socket is specified. Where vandalism is prevalent, clutch screws which can only be tightened but not loosened, or hexagonal sunk-head bolts may be preferable to the normal hexhead bolt (See Figure 3.31).

4 SITE SUPERVISION OF BRICKWORK

Having paid a great deal of money for beautiful and expensive bricks, it is only good sense to make sure that they are properly looked after on the site. However good the brickie may be, the best face of the wall will be the one where he is standing and the landscape designer should ensure that the work is carried out from the side which will show most after the wall is completed. If both sides must be perfect, then 'overhand' working must be prohibited so that the brickie works equally from both sides of the wall; this is obviously more expensive as two sets of scaffolding will be needed for high walls and two lots of mortar and bricks must be carried to the workplace. In any case, the landscape designer should always check the following points:

- The bricks ordered are the ones delivered.
- The pallets are undamaged, since a dropped pallet may cause cracked bricks which are not apparent until too late.
- Loose bricks should be unloaded and stored on a clean hard surface and not left where they can absorb site water or diesel fuel.
- Bricks from all pallets should be mixed when laid so that any under- or over-sized batches are blended equally into the wall.
- Mechanical handling of bricks is the most satisfactory; for expensive handmade facings the bricks should be shrink-wrapped on the pallet at the brickworks and remain untouched until they are used; they must *never* be tipped or thrown.
- Bricks should be protected from oil, mud, cement, water, frost and snow and strong sunshine. Bricks which are too dry or too wet will draw different amounts of moisture from the mortar, resulting in variations in strength and texture.
- Check that large numbers of broken bricks are not lying about – this

indicates careless handling. Up to 20 per cent of bricks may be wasted by a bad contractor, and this wastage may be looked for in the final account item headed 'extras'.

- New brickwork must be protected from rain, sun, and frost until properly set. Brickwork should be firm after seven days, but the mortar does not achieve full strength for twenty-eight days and no loading should be placed on the wall until then. Work should be stopped and the newly laid wall protected when the temperature falls to 3° C and not started until the temperature has risen to 5°. Any mortar which is still soft after seven days must be assumed to be frost damaged. Frost-damaged brickwork may have the joints raked out to a depth of 15 mm and re-pointed if the damage is only slight, but if the damage is severe the landscape designer must absolutely insist that the work be taken down and rebuilt. A thermometer (or on very important jobs a thermograph) should be placed conspicuously on site and daily records should be kept. In case of disputes over frost-damaged brickwork, the Courts will usually accept evidence on temperature figures from the nearest meteorological station.

- High freestanding walls should be braced and guarded for three days minimum until they have set – even a badly driven wheelbarrow can jar a new wall while the mortar has not yet taken its final set and cause hidden cracking which will almost certainly only reveal itself after the final account has been paid.

- Ensure that the bottoms of walls are protected from site mud and diesel splashes by placing scaffold boards on edge against them.

- Do not allow the walls to be used as a latrine – the stains are irremovable.

- Brickwork should not be built more than one metre high per day in order to avoid overloading the lower courses before the mortar has set.

- The correct amount of additives should be used; too much plasticizer or retarder will affect the mortar quality.

- A good bricklayer will check the vertical line of his perpends every three or four courses, and he will use a 'storey rod' which is marked in brick courses to ensure that small variations in the brick thickness or the mortar bed do not accumulate over several courses, which would cause the wall to finish at the wrong height.

- Water for mixing mortar should be of drinkable quality, not containing any algal or chemical impurities which may affect the strength and chemical composition of the mortar.

- No mortar should be 'knocked up' by adding more water to a stale mix in order to render it workable.

- Mechanical mixers, banker boards, and spot boards on which mortar is mixed and kept at the workplace should be cleaned thoroughly between batches of mortar, since fragments of partly set mortar hasten the setting of the new batch. If the mortar colour is changed between batches, traces of the previous colour will mar the later batch.

- Gates and heavy items to be fixed to the brickwork should preferably not be fixed until the brick wall has achieved its full strength at 28 days, and lighter items should not be fixed till seven days after completion.

These points are admittedly the direct responsibility of the contractor and the clerk of works, but the landscape designer should make it clear to the contractor that he is aware of the principles of good workmanship and site practice and that he intends to see them carried out; it is far easier to establish good site discipline by demonstrating a thorough knowledge of the subject at the outset of the job than to attempt remedial work at a later date.

5 NATURAL AND MAN-MADE STONE WALLING

The term masonry used to be construed as that branch of building in which the construction was stone and it rarely applied to bricklaying. Now, however, the term is applied equally to both.

5.1   NATURAL STONE

In most areas of the UK where stone is an indigenous material, its use in buildings, boundary walls and so forth forms a traditional part of masonry construction. In the days when labour was cheap and the material to hand, farming folk would put their local stone to all manner of uses; perhaps some of the most spectacular are to be found on Dartmoor where granite was worked to provide all types of walls, bridges, doorways and gate posts as well as the staddle stones for keeping the damp and rodents from their stored corn and the mortars for grinding it. Even the early tramways built from the quarry to the nearest road were often made from granite and it was over a set of these rails that the huge granite blocks bearing the City arms at either end of London Bridge were transported from Heytor Quarry. It is great fun trying to track down the origins of stonework in London and the other big towns and cities, and it gives the landscape designer a greater respect for the material and the men who quarried it, worked it and transported it to its final destination.

However, the art of stone masonry must not be considered as a dead art, as even today the landscape designer may be lucky enough to work on a prestigious contract where natural stone is called for, or within a National Park, AONB or other conservation area where the local planning authority can insist on the use of natural stone or, at the very least, artificial stone. It is not easy to calculate the structural strength of stone walls, especially those made of unsquared stone, as the nature of the stone itself, the variation in joint thickness, and chemical reactions in the stone and adjacent materials all affect the strength of the wall. As a rough guide, walls with well-fitting stones laid in lime mortar have a strength of about 75 per cent of an equivalent brick wall, and walls made of rough stones have a strength of about 50 per cent of the equivalent brick wall.

Natural stone is expensive, beautiful and durable when properly laid, and it weathers well; but because of its cost, walls in buildings are often built with stone faces and brick backs. Building stone for external walls in the UK is either limestone (calcium carbonate), sandstone (quartz) or granite (igneous).

Those seeking suitable stone for specific projects should refer to the 1991 *Natural Stone Directory* published by Ealing Publications at £25.00. This is a new edition which covers all British quarries, and also lists importers of foreign stone; it contains coloured illustrations and gives the characteristics of the stone abstracted from each quarry. The main groups of natural stones indigenous to the UK and most commonly used for walling are as follows:

- *Portland stone*: grey-white, hard limestone; smooth, with shell flecking.
- *York stone*: more often used for paving, yellow-buff, shows laminations clearly.
- *Cotswold stone*: grey-buff limestone in smaller sizes than Portland; splits easily.
- *Bath stone*: creamy-buff; softer; smooth textured; not strongly marked.
- *Granite*: pink or grey; sparkling; unlaminated igneous stone; hard to cut; and virtually indestructible.

When the choice of stone is left to the landscape designer, it is important to remember that the final weathered colour is likely to change after a few years' exposure to the elements and pollutants. For example, limestone is slightly soluble in acid rain so that it weathers unevenly, becoming darker in sheltered parts and washing paler in exposed parts, while sandstone is less soluble and retains its original colour better. Granite being practically impervious does not change its appearance much, if at all. An imported stone which appears to be similar to the local stone may change its appearance considerably during the course of weathering, and although this may not matter for a detached freestanding wall, it is an important consideration when repairing or matching existing stonework. Stone which is native to inland areas should not be used in coastal areas; stone from a dry district should not be used in areas of heavy rainfall, and stone from mild frost-free climates should not be used where there is frost risk, since weathering may be excessive and the stone may even disintegrate. Two or more kinds of stone should never be mixed in the same wall, as chemical reactions may occur between them. Limestone is liable to leach and stain other stones or brickwork if it is subjected to present day acid rain run-off, and if limestone must be used in conjunction with other building materials, great care must be taken in the design of drips, throatings, DPCs and coping details. These recommendations also apply to cast or reconstructed stone, as the aggregate is natural stone dust or fine aggregate which will react with atmospheric conditions and other building materials in the same way as natural stones. Man-made stone will behave in the same way as concrete. (See Figure 5.1c).

The best way to understand masonry is to keep notes on the way existing walls in a similar stone have been built and are weathering. After a while, keeping notes and making little sketches or taking photographs will cease to become a chore, and like all aspects of hard and soft landscape it will become absorbed into a general pool of knowledge that can be drawn upon when necessary.

Some aspects of natural stonework can really only be understood by long experience working with the material. For example, newly quarried stone contains some 'quarry sap' which enables it to be worked easily, and may make the stone rather vulnerable until it has been weathered; also occasionally the salts in Portland cement mortar or the backing brickwork can set up a reaction in the stone which eventually causes scaling and flaking. The best way to check this type of information is to rely on local knowledge gleaned from master masons, local building inspectors from the local authority and so forth. Only the quarry-master can tell whether a stone is fit to be worked or to be handled after working. Large ashlar stones have to be handled by lifting gear which can damage the stone if it is still soft when moved. In the case of walls built of large ashlar blocks which cannot be re-shaped on site the contractor or his mason should check the stone sizes and shapes before laying them, even to the extent of having the wall laid dry as a complete check on all stone sizes if the wall is an important feature (See Figure 5.1a).

Walling stone

There are three main finishes to stone walls and five types of walling likely to be met in landscape work. The finishes are divided into three categories to express the work that the mason will have to do to the stone as delivered from the quarry, as follows:

- Uncut or quarry-pitched stone, dressed with a hammer in the quarry or on site to remove projections.
- Roughly squared stone, shaped on site with a hammer.
- Carefully dressed stone blocks, cut to accurate sizes in the mason's yard, either by hand with hammer and chisel or, more usually, cut with very large diameter saws in the quarry works to a range of standard sizes. (Dressed stone for buildings may have a number of 'labours' put on it, ranging from simple grooving with a special chisel to elaborate 'boasted and drove' margins with raised panels of ornamental reticulation, but these expensive finishes are unlikely to be used in landscape work.) (See Figure 5.1b).

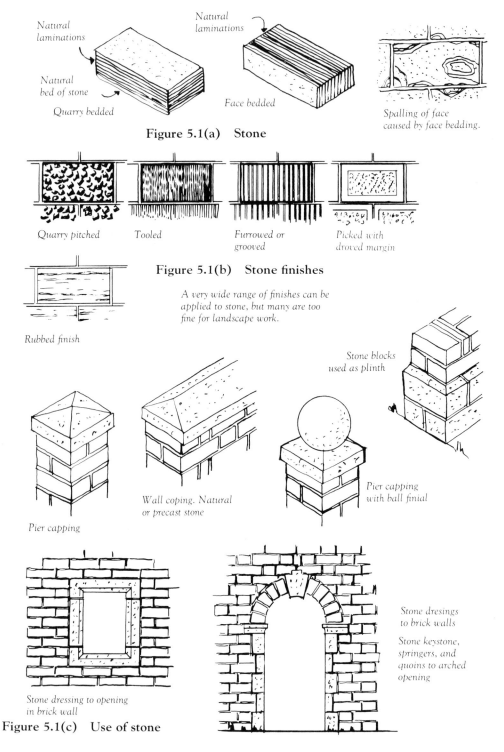

Natural
laminations

Natural
laminations

Natural
bed of stone

Quarry bedded

Face bedded

Spalling of face
caused by face bedding.

Figure 5.1(a)   Stone

Quarry pitched

Tooled

Furrowed or
grooved

Picked with
droved margin

Figure 5.1(b)   Stone finishes

*A very wide range of finishes can be
applied to stone, but many are too
fine for landscape work.*

Rubbed finish

Stone blocks
used as plinth

Pier capping

Wall coping. Natural
or precast stone

Pier capping
with ball finial

Stone dressing to opening
in brick wall

Figure 5.1(c)   Use of stone

Stone dresings
to brick walls

Stone keystone,
springers, and
quoins to arched
opening

92

Plate 12   Natural stone walling   *Building a drystone wall or dyke. Most common in limestone districts where naturally laminated stone is plentiful. The technique of drystone walling is now taught in rural crafts centres, and skilled wallers are available. These walls were made for separating fields, and they are best used in rural projects: they do not blend well with brick or formal stonework, and the dry construction makes them vulnerable to damage. Where walkers are likely to cross them, stiles or gates should be provided.*

The five types of walling describe the actual finished masonry wall; these are:

1   Uncoursed random rubble
2   Random rubble brought to courses
3   Uncoursed squared rubble
4   Snecked squared rubble
5   Coursed squared rubble
6   Ashlar

In addition there are the various types of natural drystone walling or dyking which are mostly used in conservation work and country park projects.

Plate 13   Natural stone walling   *A Scottish drystone wall showing the interlocking stones. It is the interlock between the various shaped stones which gives the wall its strength.*

Uncoursed random rubble

This, as its name implies, involves the use of uncut or very roughly cut stone of varying sizes and shapes laid as they come to hand, without horizontal courses or vertically aligned perpends. It makes good use of the smaller stones, though larger stones should be distributed through the wall to insure a good bond. Very little work, other than squaring off the odd corner with a walling hammer (quarry pitching), is required in preparing the stones; this makes it the cheapest natural stone wall available to the landscape designer. Random rubble walls are often finished with brickwork in piers, jambs to openings and in copings in order to provide true vertical and horizontal surfaces. Random rubble gives a soft-textured walling suitable for domestic scale garden walls, and takes up changes in level and direction very satisfactorily; it can also be worked round existing rock outcrops. As the joints will vary considerably in thickness they should be struck flush with no attempt to emphasize them, and the colour of the mortar should blend with the stone.

Plate 14   Natural stone walling Flint walling   *Some of the flints are 'knapped', or split to produce an even face, and some are left 'as dug' with the weathered surface of the flint showing. Flint is extremely durable, requires no maintenance, and is very difficult to damage, making it suitable for locations such as low walls to car parks.*

Where very large joints over 20 mm wide occur they can be filled with 'galleting' which consists of small pieces of matching or contrasting stone set in the joint. Gilbert White reports that in his village of Selborne, a visitor asked why the walls were 'fastened with tenpenny nails', and this is exactly what galleting looks like. Because of the type of stones used, it is not possible to produce a thin wall fair-faced both sides, and a thickness of between 300 and 460 mm is required to provide a satisfactory finish. Where brickwork is to marry into the wall a suitable brick dimension within these limits should be used (See Figure 5.2).

Random rubble brought to courses
This type of walling is very similar to squared rubble, but it consists of stones random in length and height, but brought to a regular horizontal plane every

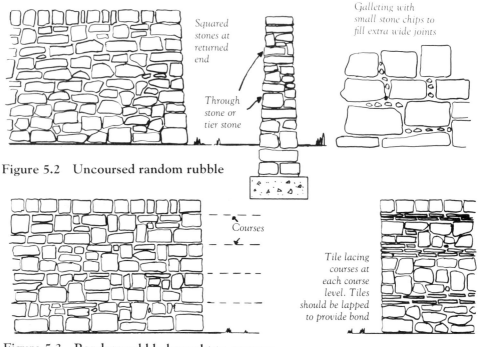

Squared stones at returned end

Through stone or tier stone

Galleting with small stone chips to fill extra wide joints

Figure 5.2   Uncoursed random rubble

Courses

Tile lacing courses at each course level. Tiles should be lapped to provide bond

Figure 5.3   Random rubble brought to courses

Joints more even thickness than random rubble

Figure 5.4   Uncoursed squared rubble

Squared rubble with brick coping and brick dressing at quoins

Snecks introduced to form stronger bond

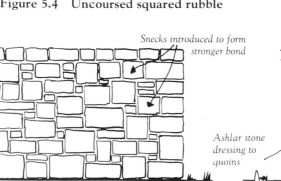

Ashlar coping

Ashlar stone dressing to quoins

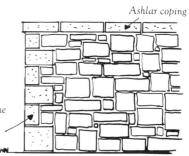

Figure 5.5   Snecked squared rubble

Plate 15   Uncoursed random rubble   *A Scottish garden wall. The stones are irregular in size and shape, though where the stone has a flat bed this is laid horizontally. The arched wall on the right is constructed of squared coursed rubble, with all stones laid to course, but with the courses varying in thickness.*

three courses or so. The courses vary in height according to the stones being used, but a height of 300 to 500 mm is usual. The appearance is more formal than squared rubble, and when the larger-sized stones are used it gives a tough appearance to the wall. The Romans used this type of walling for more permanent forts and inserted two or three courses of tiles at intervals to bring the rubble to course, which gives a strong horizontal effect to the wall (See Figure 5.3).

97

Plate 16   Rubble wall   *Exeter City wall. This shows several different types of rubble walling, built over many centuries in varying forms as money and skill dictated at the time. The centre base of the wall is built of squared coursed rubble, neatly laid; immediately above this are a few courses of snecked rubble. To the left, random rubble has been used, with some slight evidence of an attempt to bring it to courses, while the upper part of the wall is composed of very random rubble badly laid, and probably built hastily in fear of an assault on the walls.*

Uncoursed squared rubble

This is also constructed of mixed sizes of stones, but the vertical and horizontal bedding faces are squared off to give true horizontal and vertical joints. Squared rubble walls are traditionally used for farmhouse walls or town walls where random rubble presents too rural an appearance, but where cost does not allow for ashlar. These walls can still be seen surrounding the well-appointed kitchen gardens of large country houses. Where it is to be used by the landscape designer today, it is particularly suitable for courtyard walls in countryside centres and similar situations (See Figure 5.4).

Snecked squared rubble

When squared rubble is 'snecked' small rectangular or square stones are introduced to fill a 'sneck' or gap between the adjacent stones. This is not an

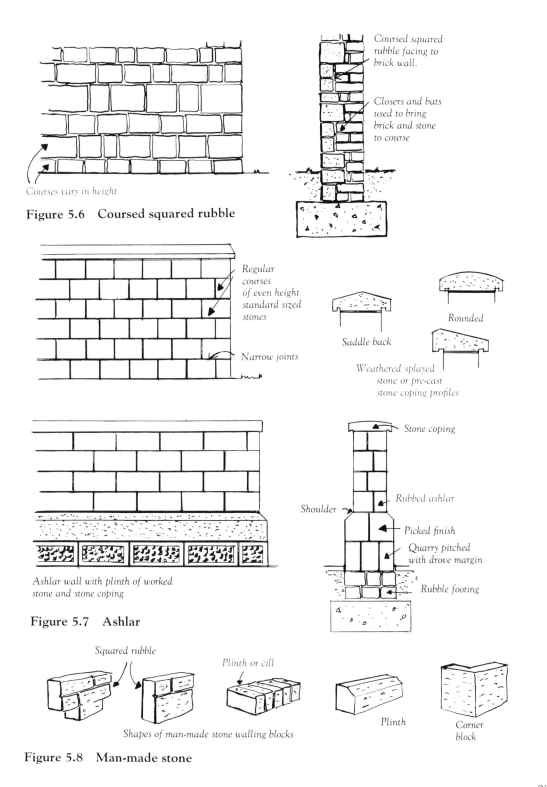

Coursed squared rubble facing to brick wall.

Closers and bats used to bring brick and stone to course

Courses vary in height

Figure 5.6   Coursed squared rubble

Regular courses of even height standard sized stones

Narrow joints

Saddle back

Rounded

Weathered splayed stone or pre-cast stone coping profiles

Stone coping

Shoulder

Rubbed ashlar

Picked finish

Quarry pitched with drove margin

Rubble footing

Ashlar wall with plinth of worked stone and stone coping

Figure 5.7   Ashlar

Squared rubble

Plinth or cill

Shapes of man-made stone walling blocks

Plinth

Corner block

Figure 5.8   Man-made stone

easy wall to build well, as it does require a skilled mason to produce a good wall without wasting a lot of material. However, when it is well designed and built it produces a strong attractive wall of sturdy appearance. Also, as it uses up the small trimmings from the larger stones, it is a useful type of walling for an expensive stone (See Figure 5.5).

Coursed squared rubble

When rubble walling is squared and coursed it gives the nearest appearance to ashlar. Each course of stones are uniform in height, but vary in length. Neat mortar joints – flush, weathered, recessed or 'mason's' – may be used in this type of walling. The stones may be only roughly dressed or given a better finish, and the completed wall gives a strong formal effect which is suitable for large scale construction associated with civil engineering work. When the stones are massive enough to require mechanical handling the walling is usually called 'block in course' and is used for heavy engineering work such as bridge abutments and canal or harbour wharfs (See Figure 5.6).

Ashlar

Ashlar is the most expensive type of walling where the stone is cut to very smooth and exact faces so that the mortar joints are kept to the minimum thickness. Only the best fine freestone is used for ashlar work, as the labour involved would be wasted on inferior material. The stones are a standard size for each wall and are larger than rubble; Portland stone may be cut in blocks up to 450 × 900 mm or even larger. Ashlar work is the most sophisticated stone walling, suitable for very high-class work in urban projects, and it is always used where mouldings form part of the stonework design; it is also used as a finish to rubble walls at gateways, piers, and arches (See Figure 5.7). Natural stone ashlar may be 'dressed', or face finished, in several ways:

- *Sawn*; the face as left by the stone saw which does not make the best of the natural stone appearance but is cheap.
- *Dragged*; the stone is brought to a true face with a rough grinder.
- *Tooled*; various tools are used across the face of the stone to produce regular or irregular grooving of varying depths.
- *Rubbed*; the stone is ground to a perfectly smooth regular face which shows off the nature of the grain.
- *Polished* stone is used for internal stonework, and is therefore unlikely to be used for landscape walls except in atria or covered courtyards. The polishing process involves bringing the stone to a reflective finish.

5.2   MAN-MADE STONE

Because of the high cost of natural stone, many local planning authorities in conservation areas, AONBs, National Parks and other protected areas will accept man-made stone as a substitute for the local natural stone, and many manufacturers specialize in producing simulated rubble or ashlar walling based on the types of natural stone walling described above. Man-made stone may be described as 'reconstructed stone', 'artificial stone', 'cast stone' or similar terms (See Figure 5.8).

Simulated Stone

The landscape designer should make quite sure which of the two main types of man-made stone he is being offered. These are:

1 Stone made of crushed natural stone aggregate with white or coloured cement binder; this merits the name of 'cast' or 'reconstructed' stone.
2 Stone made of precast concrete with colours and textures added at the casting stage. It is inaccurate to call these types 'cast' or 'reconstructed' stone; they are concrete blocks and should be treated as such.

Blocks with artificial colour added do not weather to a natural shade, but those composed of crushed stone aggregate have at least a resemblance to the stone from which they are derived. All vary considerably in quality, but where some economy is required, a well-made block manufactured from a crushed natural stone from a specific quarry can provide a reasonable compromise between the very expensive natural stone block and plain coloured concrete.

All types of man-made stone are regarded by the Building Regulations as precast concrete and tested accordingly. Structural precast concrete blocks for building construction are controlled by BS 6073: Part 1: 1981, with an average crushing strength of 25 kN/mm^2, and are therefore quite strong enough for landscape wall construction. Man-made stone has the advantage over natural stone in being consistent in size and shape as well as being considerably cheaper. Most firms produce a full range of facings, lintols, short and long plinths, copings, and plain and squint quoin blocks, all are compatible with brick dimensions. Where these are used, it makes it possible to construct 'stone' landscape walls without the services of a skilled mason. The traditional finishes of quarry pitching, hammer-dressing, and various kinds of tooling can be supplied, and it is also possible to obtain complete well-designed traditional door surrounds, window frames, and arches which can be used to enhance prestige landscape walls at a fraction of the cost of natural stone masonry.

As mentioned earlier, each manufacturer produces his own variants based on the traditional types of natural stone walling described above, and in order to give consistency to the project, the landscape designer should ensure that the choice of stone types and their accessories are available from one manufacturer. Typical sizes of man-made stone are given in Table 5.1. Each manufacturer makes a slightly different range of sizes and finishes. It is advisable to select the type and finish of block first before dimensioning the landscape wall and to work to block sizes wherever possible, since these blocks are

101

Table 5.1
Man-made stone sizes

Simulated squared rubble

200, 225, 250, 275, 300, 325 mm long
75, 100, 125, and 150 mm high
100 mm bed thickness

Simulated tooled ashlar

300, 450, 800 mm long
75, 103, 150, and 225 mm high
100 mm bed thickness

Typical lintol sizes	Clear span	Maximum uniformly distributed load
143 × 102 mm or	767 mm	3.20 kN/mm2
219 × 102 mm	919	3.66
	1072	4.12
	1224	4.57
	1376	5.03
	1529	5.49

given their face in the mould and do not present the same finish on cut surfaces. In addition to the standard sizes, manufacturers will produce special shapes such as corbels and pier caps to order to match their standard ranges, but these are expensive unless long production runs are required. However, when they are to be used the landscape designer should again ensure that all these selected accessories are available from one manufacturer.

The appearance of the finished face of these blocks depends on the colours of the aggregate and cement used and the finish applied to the face. The best versions are cast from moulds taken from a range of natural stones, and bear a close resemblance to the original except that the pattern is repeated at regular intervals. It is worth noting that the weathering of the concrete block will nevertheless be completely different from that of the natural stone. The natural stone colours most usually imitated are limestone (grey-white), York stone (yellow-buff), sandstone (reddish), granite (grey), and Portland stone (white), Cotswold stone (buff-grey) and sometimes pink granite (pink). Although finishes are usually cast in the mould, work can be applied to the blocks after casting; this may include:

● Fine close-textured rubbed surface similar to dressed stone.

- Ribbed tooled face; fine or bold ribs.
- Split face, where the block is split after casting, producing a face similar to a natural rock face.

Precast concrete garden walling blocks

The types available from garden centres, these blocks are much less attractive than man-made stone and are mostly used for garden work where cost is of prime importance. They are not controlled by any British Standard and should not be used for walls much above 600 mm high as there is no way of knowing their structural strength. There are a wide range of types available which represent Cotswold, Lakeland, Durham, or York stone, and they are cast into shapes which purport to resemble that of the natural stone as quarried. Some blocks are cast as a single unit with simulated small stone joints marked on the surface in order to save labour and skill in building the wall, and their chief use, is in small self-build work within suburban gardens.

5.3   LAYING NATURAL STONE AND MAN-MADE STONE WALLS

Since the object of the concrete (or cast stone) block is to imitate natural stonework, there is little difference in the methods of constructing landscape walls of these two materials. The main difference in them lies in the need to lay natural stone on its proper bed; that is, the way it lay in the quarry. 'Quarry-bedding' is absolutely critical if the stone is not to spall off in frosty weather or under load, and a sharp eye should be kept on the work to ensure that stones are not accidentally 'face-bedded' or laid on the face which would be exposed in the quarry. Any landscape designer who intends to include much stonework in his design should visit the quarry to see how the bed lies, since with some freestones (that is, stone without very definite bedding planes) the quarry bed is not obvious and quarry inspection will help to make this clear. Granite, being an igneous rock, does not have bedding planes, nor, of course, do unfaced man-made stones. Natural stone cannot be produced to order as can man-made stone and large quantities may have to be ordered well in advance to allow for normal quarrying procedures.

In general, the principles for the construction at the head and foot of a stone wall are similar to those used for brickwork, and the landscape designer should refer to the relevant sections for details of copings, damp-proof courses, movement joints and foundations.

Mortars for man-made stone are the same as for brickwork, and the landscape designer should refer to the information in that section in order to select a suitable mix. Mortars for natural stonework vary according to the type of stone; as a guide the following mixes are given:

- *Granite and other igneous rocks*: requires a strong 1:3 cement:sand mortar, but, granite being non-absorbent, less than the normal amount of water should be used in the mix.
- *Hard sandstones*: use 1:1:6 cement:lime:sand mortar.
- *Soft sandstone*: use 1:3:12 cement:lime:sand.
- *Copings, plinths and other ornamental features*: use 1:2:9 cement:lime:sand.
- *Very soft absorbent stone*: use 1:2½ hydraulic lime:sand.

For ashlar work a 5 mm joint is usual, while rougher walling will have joints varying from 5 mm to 15 mm according to the shape of the stones; gaps over 20 mm should be filled with small stone slips called 'galleting'. Cast stone and concrete blocks should not be pointed but jointed as the work proceeds. The shape of the joint should be consistent with the type of walling since a very formal joint such as a mason's or weathered joint does not suit the varying thickness of mortar found in random rubble walling; for example:

- Ashlar usually has a very narrow smooth slightly recessed or flush joint which is intended to be nearly invisible.
- Heavy block rubble walling used in engineering work often has a mason's joint which emphasizes the strong appearance.
- The rougher types of rubble walling look best with flush struck or struck and dragged joints to give an informal appearance.

6 FENCES

Fences are frequently regarded as a cheap or short-term alternative to walls, but they have many advantages over solid walls excluding the financial benefits. The advantages of a well-designed fence include the following points:

- Open fences form an inconspicuous barrier where the eye travels through the barrier rather than being completely stopped by it – the most fully developed form of this is the ha-ha fence.
- Fences provide better security than low or medium-height walls where this is required, since wire fences prevent the concealment of intruders, and even a low fence is more difficult to climb than a low wall.
- Except for the close-boarded types of fence, there is more light penetration to support planting of non-shade loving plants.
- When erected inside a hedge, the wire fence provides an invisible barrier which prevents stock and people from pushing gaps through the hedge and also protects the hedge itself in its development stage.
- Fences, unlike walls, can be moved or altered easily during the lifetime of the project, or even during the contract stage if the client or the local authority has a change of heart.
- Repairs and maintenance to fences are generally less costly than for walls though the maintenance will have to be carried out more frequently, since timber which is preservative treated or painted should be maintained every three years and every two years in corrosive or saline atmospheres. Fences are also more easily damaged than walls and the condition of line wires, tensioning devices and wire mesh will have to be checked at least once a year and more often where children are playing or where sports activities are carried on.
- Fences, especially open-pattern fences, create less sense of enclosure than the equivalent height wall, so that small spaces may be divided without appearing claustrophobic while still providing security.
- Open timber fences are more suited to rural and semi-rural situations

105

such as country-centre car parks, while still providing substantial barriers to stock and vehicles.

- Timber board fences can be designed to give directional privacy without fully obstructing the view.
- In closely developed housing sites, a fence and its supports occupies less ground than a wall with its foundations and piers; this may be a consideration with developers who are seeking to make the most economical use of the land.
- An open fence allows the owner more choice of planting, the option of covering it with climbers or ramblers.
- Timber, chain-link and metal fencing can be stained or painted in a wide range of colours to suit the building design or the building owner's taste; for example, company colours, university colours, or racing colours can be selected.
- Where high visibility is an advantage, metal and timber rails or posts can be painted with brilliant white or reflective paint, while bright yellow or orange can be used to indicate danger areas.

It may seem that there is very little to consider in the client's brief on the subject of fencing, which is taken here to include gates, railings, and all other types of fencing, but there are a number of factors which should be agreed with the client before fence types are specified, and although each project will have different requirements the following points are typical of many contracts:

- *Security*   The most critical is security. Are the boundary and internal fences intended to keep the public in or out? Are intruders a mild nuisance or a serious threat to the property? Perhaps a 1.8 m fence with one line of barbed wire and a field gate with a padlock may suffice, or it may be necessary to call in a security specialist who will design an electronic security system allied to 3.5 m high-tensile welded fencing with electronically controlled gates. The cost of very secure fencing is high so it is important to get the budget allocation for security correct at the outset. If the landscape designer does not consider security seriously he may leave the client vulnerable to expensive depredations, whether caused by theft or vandalism.

- *Function*   The work which the fence is called on to perform must be stated. The effect on the fencing of large stock, active adults, animals, vehicles or children will dictate the type and construction of the fence. A fence which has to contain one-ton Charolais bulls and keep out rabbits and inquisitive children will be completely different from one which has to demarcate car parking while imparting a rural character to the project and allowing walkers to climb over it.

- *Legal constraints*   Any legal restraints on the height or type of fencing must be ascertained. Planning permission may be needed for boundary fences in Conservation Areas and other protected areas and the local planning authority may impose conditions as part of the landscape design control which is usually dealt with in the 'reserved matters' part of planning permission. The highway authorities may impose limitations on fences where they border a highway and especially where sight lines at junctions are involved. In some private estates there are controls on the type and height of fences which may be erected even in private gardens and there may also be covenants on the land which affect the fencing. Local authorities usually have standard specifications for projects such as schools, housing estates, and parks which must be followed.

- *Emergency access*   The section on Gates deals with access by emergency vehicles but the landscape designer should remember to discuss the type and position of gates with the fire brigade, the police and the ambulance service at an early stage in the project.

- *Animal-proof fences*   If wild animals form part of the attraction in a country park there are regulations governing zoos which may be applicable to the fencing. The keeping of lions and tigers requires very special fencing indeed. Dog breeding, horse breeding, kennels, and riding establishments all have to be licensed by the local authority and they may impose conditions on the fencing design and construction.

- *Maintenance costs*   The timing and cost of maintenance operations may be an important consideration to the client and his maintenance schedule should be agreed before the fencing is selected.

- *Negligence*   Whether or not the client asks for safety or security fencing it must be remembered that the Health and Safety at Work Act 1974 (c.37) and the Occupier's Liability Acts 1957(c.31) and 1984(c.3) place a duty of care on the owner and/or occupier, so that failure to protect the occupants, the workforce or the public at large from foreseeable hazards is an offence, and the negligent landscape designer may find himself in considerable trouble if he has not considered the problems of hazards carefully. The Acts also apply to sites under construction. Further guidelines are given in the sections on Playgrounds and Protective Barriers.

British Standards cover fencing in great detail, and they include a series of standardized fences with reference numbers which can be used to specify a fence type without further detail. It is not, however, sufficient to specify a fence 'to be to BS 1722: Pt3, type XXX'; as there are many options in the Standards, and the landscape designer must list those sections in the Standard which he wishes to incorporate into the specification. He should also be quite certain that he does indeed require the fence to comply in every aspect, since there are many occasions where a better quality fence or a cheaper substitute would be more appropriate than the BS specification.

6.1   WIRE BOUNDARY FENCING

The most commonly used types are plain post-and-wire (also known as stob-and-wire); chain-link on timber, steel, or concrete posts; stock fencing of various patterns, and combinations of these. There are also special boundary fences such as rabbit-stop and deer-stop fences which are used to guard planting where these animals are present in pest proportions. For fences not required to withstand heavy usage, post centres of 3 m are usual, though for light plain post-and-wire fencing 3.5 m is acceptable and security fences which are usually 2.4 m high or more may need posts at 1600 mm centres or even closer so that the fence cannot be ruptured by ramming. If 'droppers' (also called 'prick posts') are used the spacing of posts for light wire fencing may be extended. Droppers are light posts which are fixed to the line wires but are not fixed into the ground, and which help to brace the line wires without incurring the expense of full-sized posts.

Post and wire

Plain post-and-wire fencing is covered in British Standard 1722:Pt 3, and is used for temporary boundaries, light stock control, and hedge protection. It is very cheap and rapidly erected and consists of two or three lines of plain galvanized or plastic-coated galvanized wire stapled to timber posts, and there may be an extra low level wire to deter stock. Plain mild steel (carbon steel) galvanized wire is manufactured in 1.6, 2.0, 2.5, 3.15, 4.0 and 5.0 mm diameter sizes with the choice of size depending on the expected loading. The top wire which takes most of the strain should be at least 3.15 mm while the lower wires may be 2.5 mm thick for ordinary field and estate work. The lighter sizes are suitable for gardens and hedge reinforcement and the heavier ones are used for cattle and horse fences and for housing estates where children have scant respect for boundaries. Other types of wire suitable for wire fences are high-tensile steel, spring steel, plastic-coated high-tensile steel and plastic-coated spring steel, though the last should only be used with droppers. Straining posts are usually 150 m apart and even 300 m apart if high-tensile wire is used, with intermediate posts at 3 m or 3.5 m centres. If a dropper fence is specified the droppers are cleft chestnut, 50 × 25 mm battens or steel flats at 2 m centres, and their use allows the intermediate posts to be placed at 12 m centres with the straining posts at 300 m centres. Droppers may be short lengths spanning two wires only or full-height drop-pers spanning all the wires, and their purpose is to extend the space between posts and to prevent people or stock bunching the wires and squeezing through them (See Figure 6.1).

BS 1722:Part 3 gives a choice of standard fence types ranging from 900, 1050, 1200, and 1350 mm high for general purposes to 1800 mm and 2100 mm high for greater protection, and the Standard also gives the proper spacing of the line wires which must be closer together at the bottom than the top with gaps from 100 mm to 330 mm. The top wire should not be less than 75 mm below the top of the post. The BS reference numbers indicate the type of fence: SC = concrete posts; DC = dropper pattern with concrete posts; SS = steel posts; DS = dropper pattern with concrete posts; SW = wooden posts; DW = dropper pattern with wooden posts. The heights are given by adding the figure in millimetres, and the wire spacing is indicated by the suffix A, B, or C. A fence 1.05 m high on steel posts with five wires at 250, 250, 230, and 150 mm apart is SS105A. (See Figure 6.1).

Forestry fencing

For simple forestry fencing designed to restrain public and stock access to plantations, stob-and-wire fencing about 1 m high which consists of treated natural round posts 75 mm diameter at 5 m centres driven 500 mm into the ground, with three lines of 3 mm plain galvanized wire, is quite adequate. There are two more special types of fence which may be required in a landscape contract in a rural or semi-rural situation, these are the rabbit-stop fence and the deer-stop fence. (See Figure 6.2).

Rabbit-stop fencing

Rabbit fencing is essential for the protection of newly planted woodland or ornamental shrubs where rabbits are a pest and it consists of 1200 mm × 31mm mesh galvanized wire netting on two 2.5 mm line wires, 900 mm high with 150 mm buried below ground 150 mm down and turned outwards from the protected area. The fence is supported by 75 mm diameter treated softwood posts at 4 m centres and driven 700 mm into firm ground or set in concrete footings if the ground is very weak, with straining posts and struts as for standard wire fences. (See Figure 6.2)

Deer-stop fencing

In the South of England and Midlands deer fencing may be needed to protect planting against attack by roe, fallow, and other small deer especially in large open tracts such as the New Forest where deer are a major cause of garden damage, since they have a passion for expensive and uncommon roses. The most suitable fence for this purpose is a field fencing of high tensile rectangular mesh 1800 mm high which is manufactured for protection against the smaller deer and is supported on 100 mm diameter natural treated softwood posts, 2400 mm long, driven 600 mm into firm ground at 3 m centres; straining posts and struts should be 150 mm diameter. On Exmoor and in the

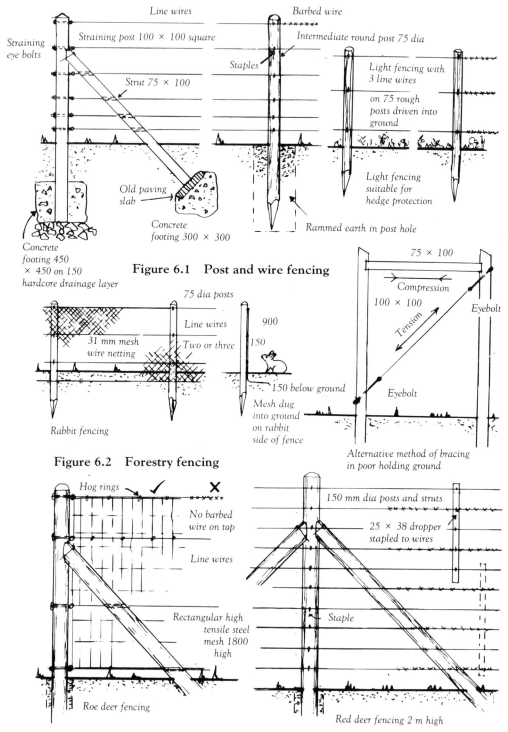

Figure 6.1 Post and wire fencing

Straining eye bolts

Line wires

Straining post 100 × 100 square

Barbed wire

Intermediate round post 75 dia

Staples

Strut 75 × 100

Light fencing with 3 line wires

on 75 rough posts driven into ground

Light fencing suitable for hedge protection

Old paving slab

Concrete footing 300 × 300

Rammed earth in post hole

Concrete footing 450 × 450 on 150 hardcore drainage layer

Figure 6.2 Forestry fencing

75 dia posts

Line wires

Two or three

31 mm mesh wire netting

900

150

150 below ground

Mesh dug into ground on rabbit side of fence

Rabbit fencing

75 × 100

Compression

100 × 100

Tension

Eyebolt

Eyebolt

Alternative method of bracing in poor holding ground

Hog rings

✓ ✗

No barbed wire on top

Line wires

Rectangular high tensile steel mesh 1800 high

Roe deer fencing

150 mm dia straining post and strut

150 mm dia posts and struts

25 × 38 dropper stapled to wires

Staple

Red deer fencing 2 m high

Table 6.1
British Standard wire fences

Situation	Type	Wires	Height	BS reference
Gardens, housing	plain or dropper	3	900 mm	??90
Fields, stock fencing	plain or dropper	5	1005 mm	??105A
		6	1005 mm	??105B
Large stock, highways	plain or dropper	6	1200 mm	??120
Light security highways	plain or dropper	7	1350 mm	??135A
		8	1350 mm	??135B
		9	1350 mm	??135C
Close wires for stock and security	dropper	11	1800 mm	??180
		16	2100 mm	??210

? = Complete the reference with your selection

Highlands of Scotland the red deer, which are large, strong, and powerful jumpers are a considerable nuisance as even a small herd of hungry red deer can graze and trample a garden or a plantation to the ground overnight. They are usually found in wilder countryside where forestry areas have considerable perimeters to be fenced, so therefore a cheaper fence constructed on site from local timber and coils of wire is preferable. This should be at least 2000 mm high, made of five lines of 2.5 mm galvanized line wire and five lines of two-ply galvanized barbed wire fixed to 2400 mm long, 150 mm diameter treated softwood posts driven into firm ground at 3 m centres, with 25 × 38 mm timber droppers, 1000 mm long, stapled to the wire at 1500 mm centres. The droppers are essential for deer fences round plantations, because if the cornuferous fauna are in search of the coniferous flora their antlers are apt to become trapped between loose wires. Deer ladders are provided for the keepers and foresters to cross the fence at suitable points (See Figure 6.2).

Field fencing

Field or stock fencing is a woven or welded square-mesh galvanized wire fencing material in a range of heights and mesh sizes used for containing stock, and though it is unlikely to be needed for ordinary urban and commercial landscape contracts, it should be used where farm or zoo animals are a country park attraction, and the correct type and height of field fencing for the kind of animals should be specified. This is in addition to the requirements discussed under Briefing. The main types are described in BS 1722:Pt 2:1986 which recommends appropriate sizes for various animals; all these stock fences have wires closer together at the bottom than at the top. Field fencing also makes an excellent support for young hedging, climbing plants

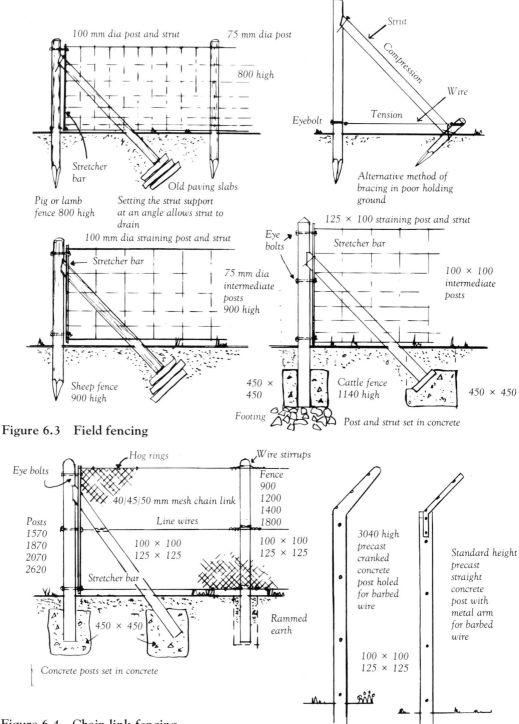

Figure 6.3   Field fencing

Figure 6.4   Chain link fencing

112

and shrubs, since the closer wires at ground level enable the plants to get a good start and they also deter children, cats, and dogs from passing through. Rabbits, hares, and muntjac deer must be restricted by wire netting (See Figure 6.3).

The British Standard references indicate: number of horizontal wires; width of the roll in cms; and spacing of vertical wires in centimetres. (See Table 6.2).

Chain Link Fencing

Chain link is the most commonly used wire fencing for housing estates and local authority parks. It is relatively unclimbable, easily and rapidly erected and available from stock almost anywhere. Its main disadvantage is that if one part is damaged the adjoining sections tend to unravel, so that repair may require the replacement of more than the original damaged portion. Chain-link mesh is specified in BS 4102:1986 and as chain-link fencing in BS 1722:Part 1:1986 and the British Standard gives detailed specifications for the wire itself, its coatings, the sizes and quality of timber, concrete and steel posts, details of all fixings required, and methods of construction. Reference numbers are given for a series of standardized heights and weights of fencing, so that the landscape designer need only quote a number to cover the height and weight of the chosen fence.

Chain-link mesh is now manufactured in an ever-increasing range of gauges, heights, finishes and colours, and ranges from lightweight 50 mm mesh material for gardens to 40 mm heavy duty (or 'railway') security fencing. The fencing wire can be supplied in galvanized, plastic-coated, or galvanized and plastic-coated forms, and in mild steel or high-tensile steel for security applications. Light plastic-coated galvanized wire is 2.65/2.0 mm thick, medium is 3.15/2.24 mm, heavy is 3.55/2.5 mm, extra heavy is 4.0/3.0 mm, and super weight is 4.75/3.55 mm (the two figures are the overall thickness of the coated wire and the actual wire thickness). The heaviest gauges are used only for security applications with smaller mesh sizes of 25 mm, 40 mm and 45 mm, but the standard mesh is 50 mm and this is suitable for most fencing purposes. The plastic coating on chain-link can be damaged, and unless the wire itself is galvanized it is likely to corrode. Plastic coating may be vulnerable to fire, and a favourite youthful game was to set two parallel fences alight and to see which burned to the end first. The chain-link mesh is fixed to the end posts by means of a stretcher bar threaded through the meshes and bolted to the post with the same eye bolts that are used to tension the line wires. The mesh is tied to the line wires as for plain wire fences and the tying wire is either aluminium, 2.0 mm plastic coated or 1.6 mm galvanized wire, and secures the chain-link at 900 mm centres, though for speed and efficiency on long runs of fencing hog rings closed with a special tool are often used for fixing mesh to line wires instead of tying wires. Hog rings or patent clips are more satisfactory than tying wires as they are fixed

113

Table 6.2
British Standard welded wire fences

Situation	Wires	Width of roll	Spacing of verticals	BS references
Pigs, lambs, roe deer	8	800 mm	150 mm	8/80/15
Roe deer, red deer (double height)	8	800 mm	300 mm	8/80/30
Sheep, red deer (double height)	6	900 mm	300 mm	6/90/30
Sheep, cattle, roe, red deer (double height)	7	1000 mm	150 mm	7/10/15
Cattle, red deer (double height)	8	1000 mm	150 mm	8/10/15
Cattle	8	1100 mm	300 mm	8/11/30

with a special tool and there is less likelihood of careless fixing; if each mesh is fixed to the line wire there is much less chance of the fence being vandalized, but this method is more expensive. Intermediate posts for chain-link fencing should be at 3 m centres, and straining posts at 69 m centres (See Figure 6.4).

The following recommendations for using chainlink fencing are based on British Standard 1722: Pt 1:1986. The BS reference numbers indicate the type of wire, (G = galvanized, P = plastic-coated), the type of post (C = concrete, S = steel, W = wooden), the height of the fence (90 = 90 mm, 120 = 120 mm); and the type of mesh is A, B, C, D, or E according to the strength of fence required; so that a fence specified as GLS120A would be a fence 120 mm high with galvanized mesh on steel posts with heavy-duty mesh suitable for playground fencing. (See Table 6.3.)

The security fences have either barbed wire at the top or extension arms with barbed wire. They must always be installed so that the projection is away from any public access route.

Ball-stop fencing

This is the name used for fencing for tennis courts, sports fields and playgrounds where ball games are played, and it is usually made of chain-link fencing on specially tall tubular, rectangular, or angle steel posts, though it is most common to specify fencing systems complete with doors and fixings which are supplied by specialist manufacturers. Where extra-high fencing is needed another two to three metres of 125 × 125 × 3 mm nylon netting may be used for the upper part of the fence to reduce loading on the posts, while for very small children's playgrounds a ball-stop fence made entirely of nylon netting would be adequate, bearing in mind that if vandalism is prevalent nylon can be burnt or slashed. A typical ball-stop fence suitable for controlled playgrounds would be constructed of light gauge 45 mm chain-link

Table 6.3
British Standard types of chain-link fencing

Situation	Type	Mesh	Height	Lines	BS reference
Gardens	light	50 mm	900 mm	2	?L?90
	medium	50 mm			?L?90A
Playgrounds	heavy	50 mm	1200 mm	3	?L?120
	extra heavy	50 mm			?L?120A
Highways and	medium	40/50 mm	1400 mm	3	?L?140
factories	heavy	40/50 mm			?L?140A
Recreation	extra heavy	50 mm			?L?140B
Railways,	medium	50 mm	1400 mm	3	?L?140C barbed top
motorways	heavy	40 mm			?L?140D barbed top
Industrial and	heavy	50 mm	1800 mm	3	?L?180
security	extra heavy	50 mm			?L?180A
	heavy	40 mm			?L?180B
Railway, extra	heavy	50 mm	1800 mm	3	?L?180C extension
security	extra heavy	50 mm			?L?180D extension
	heavy	40 mm			?L?180E extension

? = Complete the reference with your selection

mesh 3000 mm high on 4.75 mm straining wires fixed to tapered tubular steel posts set in concrete at 3 m centres. Further guidelines on playground fencing are given in the Playground Fencing section.

Tennis court surrounds are described in BS 1722: Part 13, and are always supplied complete with doors and all fixings, and are specified to enclose one, two or three standard size courts (competition courts are constructed complete by specialist contractors). A typical tennis court surround would consist of light gauge 45 mm mesh galvanized plastic-coated chain-link on 4.75 mm straining wires fixed to 45 × 45 × 5 mm mild steel angle posts and struts with a 1000 × 2000 mm gate of the same materials, complete with hinges, latch and lock. This size of gate will admit even the largest tennis player, but if access is needed for machinery, double gates will be needed. The surround would be 2460 or 2800 mm high with posts at 3.5 m centres or 3660 mm high with posts at 2.75 m centres. Where heavy and possibly rough ball game use is expected such as football or cricket practice it is better to use welded steel 62 × 66 mm mesh panels on steel posts at 2 m centres, and if there is much risk of balls travelling over the fence it may be necessary to provide cranked arms to the posts with the mesh extending 1 m into the play area. In very confined sites such as roof-top sports areas or where high-speed roads are adjacent to the ball game area it may even be necessary to roof in the space with light welded-mesh panels or nylon ball-stop netting on alloy framing, and in this case a structural engineer should be consulted (See Figure 6.5)

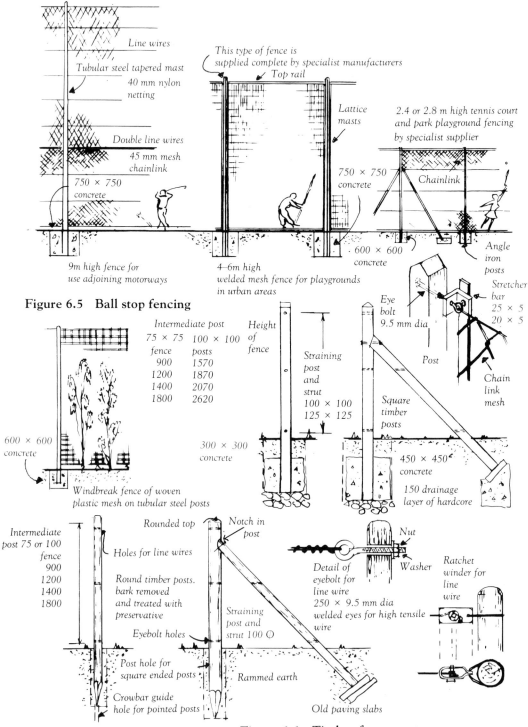

Line wires

Tubular steel tapered mast

40 mm nylon netting

This type of fence is supplied complete by specialist manufacturers

Top rail

Lattice masts

2.4 or 2.8 m high tennis court and park playground fencing by specialist supplier

Double line wires

45 mm mesh chainlink

750 × 750 concrete

750 × 750 concrete

Chainlink

9m high fence for use adjoining motorways

4–6m high welded mesh fence for playgrounds in urban areas

600 × 600 concrete

Angle iron posts

Figure 6.5   Ball stop fencing

Intermediate post		Height of fence
75 × 75 fence	100 × 100 posts	
900	1570	
1200	1870	
1400	2070	
1800	2620	

Straining post and strut 100 × 100 125 × 125

Square timber posts

Eye bolt 9.5 mm dia

Post

Stretcher bar 25 × 5 20 × 5

Chain link mesh

600 × 600 concrete

300 × 300 concrete

450 × 450 concrete

150 drainage layer of hardcore

Windbreak fence of woven plastic mesh on tubular steel posts

Intermediate post 75 or 100 fence
900
1200
1400
1800

Rounded top

Notch in post

Nut

Ratchet winder for line wire

Holes for line wires

Round timber posts. bark removed and treated with preservative

Detail of eyebolt for line wire 250 × 9.5 mm dia welded eyes for high tensile wire

Washer

Eyebolt holes

Straining post and strut 100 ⌀

Post hole for square ended posts

Rammed earth

Crowbar guide hole for pointed posts

Old paving slabs

Figure 6.6   Timber fence posts

Posts and foundations for wire fencing

As mentioned above, posts for all types of wire fencing may be timber, concrete, mild steel or high-tensile steel in angle or tube form. Timber is cheap and easily erected, since it is usually only driven into the ground, but it has a comparatively short life even when pressure impregnated with preservative. Precast reinforced concrete posts are the most frequently used alternative since they are available in a good selection of heights and various finishes and they require no maintenance; they also have the line wire holes preformed, thus saving a drilling operation on site, and unless concrete is hit with a sledge hammer or vehicle it is fairly damage resistant. Mild steel tubular section posts are used mainly for security fencing and tennis courts because of the height required (which would involve very large concrete sections), and when made in the form of high-tensile posts they are very difficult to cut or break. They are usually galvanized and/or plastic-coated for weather protection. For ordinary boundary fences up to 1500 mm high, mild steel rolled angles are used (known as 'angle irons') and these are supplied pre-drilled or notched to take the line wires, while the end and intermediate straining posts and struts are also pre-drilled for bolting together on site. Line wires are either threaded through angle irons or fixed in the notches with special clips or tying wire. Line wires are fixed to timber posts with staples which enables the wire to be erected at the later stages of the contract.

Unless the ground is stable it is preferable to set all posts, or at any rate the straining posts and their struts, in concrete footings, though if only the upper layer of ground is soft it is acceptable to use posts long enough to reach down to sound ground. The purpose of the footing is to stabilize the post, to locate it exactly where it should be, and to help it to resist lateral pull by the wire or right-angle pressure on the fence. A typical footing size for a 75 mm square or round post would be 300 × 300 × 600 or 700 mm deep depending on the stability of the soil, and for 100 × 100 mm posts footings 450 × 450 mm would be satisfactory, though if the ground is very soft the footing should be increased by 50 mm all round, or alternatively the soft patches can be excavated and replaced with weak concrete or well-rammed hardcore. Excavations of Anglo-Saxon timber dwellings show that the main posts supporting even barn-sized buildings were often stabilized by ramming large and small stones (not broken stone) firmly round the post to the bottom of the post hole, thus forming a well drained support about 100 to 200 mm larger than the post, and there is no reason why this technique should not be equally satisfactory today if there is an adequate supply of hard stones on the site. Concrete for footings is best specified by selecting a standard mix to BS 5328:1981 and the standard mix most suitable for strong footings where there is some stress on the fence is the C7P mix with 40 mm maximum-size aggregate. C7P is a 1:3:6 cement:sand:aggregate or 1:8 'all-in' (or 'as-dug ballast') mix with the proportions measured by volume and not weighed. This is stronger than necessary for light fencing with no stresses, such as field

117

fences or stob-and-wire, and a 1:10 all-in is permitted by the British Standards and will be adequate for these types, but however simple the job the concrete must be correctly mixed and poured. The cement and sand must first be mixed dry, then the coarse aggregate added and when these are thoroughly mixed the water is added to produce a soft but not sloppy mix. If the concrete is mixed by hand the traditional formula is to turn it three times dry and three times wet so that no ingredient is distinguishable. It is sometimes recommended that 100 mm to 150 mm of soil should be laid over the top of the footing as indicated in the British Standards, but unless close planting is an essential part of the landscape design a timber post bottom is better left exposed in order to prevent rotting, while a small area of exposed concrete makes a good mowing strip in grassed areas. The foot of the post should stand on a 75 mm layer of coarse gravel, broken brick, or stones and the concrete should then be poured round the post, thus allowing rainwater running down the post or flowing across the ground to drain away. The post must be supported without disturbance until the concrete has set. Timber posts may also be fixed by setting them in 'Metposts' or similar shoes, which are steel spikes with a socket at the top which will accept 75 or 100 mm square posts. The spikes are 600 mm to 900 mm long and are driven into the ground down to the socket before the post is inserted and if necessary nailed in position, and as for ordinary timber post driving, the line of the spike should be established by driving a steel bar into the ground first. These shoes form a very useful rapid fixing where access to the post hole or space for concreting is difficult, and they also permit the line of the fencing to be altered and replacement posts to be fitted more easily at a later date. Alternative types of 'Metpost' can be bolted down to existing concrete for alteration work, or cast into a new concrete slab.

Timber fence posts

The British Standards for fencing give the allowable proportion of defects in the posts, including checks, knots, resin pockets, waney edges, pinholes, slope of grain and splits, but no signs of disease or rot are permissible. As previously mentioned, the landscape designer should consider whether or not he requires the standard recommended or if a lower or higher standard is advisable for that particular job. The recommended sizes for timber fence posts according to the size and type of fence are given, but these may have to be modified if suitable timber is unavailable or if the fence is to be more heavily stressed than normal, as might be the case in a fence designed to control crowds. Timber posts are usually either round timber, or 75 × 75 mm or 100 × 100 mm treated softwood. The BS gives the minimum height of post for each fence height, but commercial posts are supplied ex-stock 1200, 1500, 1800, 2100, 2400, and 2700 mm long. Timber straining posts at the end of the fence, at intermediate points, at the gate, and at the corners are a size larger than the ordinary fencing posts (that is, 100 × 75 mm and 125 × 100 mm) and have struts bracing them against the pull of the wire which are set into a notch within the upper third of the post. The line wires are fixed to the posts and tensioned either by eye-bolts, ratchet winders (winding brackets) or, for round posts only, the wire may be pulled tightly round the post with a wire strainer and then stapled. Intermediate straining posts obviously have two struts along the line of the wire, while corner posts need two struts at right angles to each other. The struts should preferably be bolted, not nailed, to the post except for light field fencing where galvanized nails should be used. Timber posts have the advantage that they can take line wires at any heights or centres, and are more easily replaced than concrete posts since the line wires do not pass through the post. The traditional Canadian corner fence post was a whole tree trunk buried in a 1 m × 1 m × 1 m pit with cross-logs set round it in layers at right angles to each other, and such a post could be expected to strain nearly a mile of wire fence. All timber posts, even the roughest, should have their tops 'weathered' with either one cut at an angle of 45°, two cuts to form a wedge shape, four cuts to form a pyramid shape, rounded off, or capped with a hardwood or non-ferrous capping nailed on. Unless they are set in concrete, timber posts should have a guide hole driven first with a crowbar and be driven with a post rammer – never a sledge hammer. The bottom of the post is traditionally pointed with four strokes of the axe, leaving a point the size of a 20p piece, and although modern posts are machine pointed they should be cleanly cut at a moderate angle (See Figure 6.6).

Precast concrete fence posts

Standard sizes, shapes, and reinforcement for precast concrete fence posts are given in the various parts of BS 1722 on fencing, but others are available from manufacturers. Precast concrete fence posts are 100 × 125 mm in section, with rounded tops and reinforced with four light-steel reinforcing rods. Recessed posts are from 140 × 115 mm to 115 × 115 mm tapered. The end, gate, and corner posts are not tapered, and are a little larger, being 125 × 125 mm and including slots for purpose-made concrete struts on one or two sides, which are bolted to the posts on site. All posts have holes for attaching straight or cranked steel or concrete arms capable of carrying barbed wire, and some manufacturers make integral posts and arms. Intermediate posts for wire fencing should be set not more than 3 m apart with the straining posts at a maximum of 69 m apart. The BS gives the minimum heights of post for various fence heights, and commercial posts are 900, 1200, 1500, 1800 and 2100 mm long, and are perforated for two, three or four line wires according to height, though the highest slot should be not less than 75 mm from the top of the post. Concrete posts and struts are not driven but are set into holes drilled with a postholer or dug by hand, and should be stabilized with concrete footings in very soft ground or where the fence is stressed, in the same way as for timber posts. The line wires are tensioned by eye-bolts

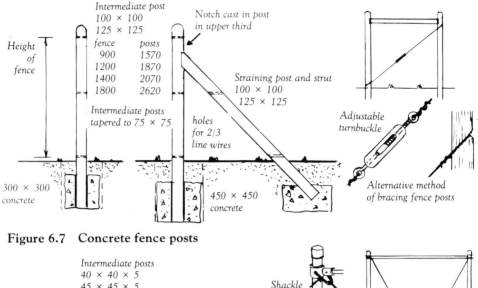

Height
of
fence

Intermediate post
100 × 100
125 × 125

fence	posts
900	1570
1200	1870
1400	2070
1800	2620

Intermediate posts
tapered to 75 × 75

Notch cast in post
in upper third

Straining post and strut
100 × 100
125 × 125

holes
for 2/3
line wires

Adjustable
turnbuckle

Alternative method
of bracing fence posts

300 × 300
concrete

450 × 450
concrete

Figure 6.7 Concrete fence posts

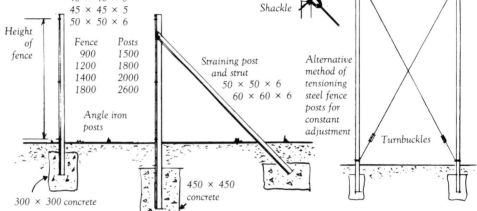

Height
of
fence

Intermediate posts
40 × 40 × 5
45 × 45 × 5
50 × 50 × 6

Fence	Posts
900	1500
1200	1800
1400	2000
1800	2600

Angle iron
posts

Shackle

Straining post
and strut
50 × 50 × 6
60 × 60 × 6

Alternative
method of
tensioning
steel fence
posts for
constant
adjustment

Turnbuckles

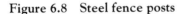

300 × 300 concrete

450 × 450
concrete

Figure 6.8 Steel fence posts

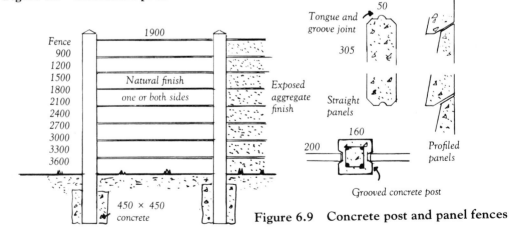

Fence
900
1200
1500
1800
2100
2400
2700
3000
3300
3600

1900

Natural finish
one or both sides

Exposed
aggregate
finish

Tongue and
groove joint

50

305

Straight
panels

160

200

Profiled
panels

Grooved concrete post

450 × 450
concrete

Figure 6.9 Concrete post and panel fences

120

passed through the straining posts and they are fastened to intermediate posts either with stirrups (light wire loops passed round the post) or hairpin staples passed round the wire and through the holes, or they may be threaded through the posts. Where the fence is subject to irregular strains (people climbing over the fence or stacking heavy material against it) it is preferable to use ratchet winders which are easily adjusted. Ratchet winders or winding brackets are small windlasses fitted to one end of the line wire, onto which the slack wire is wound, and they also have the advantage that in case of a break in the wire slack can be let out, the join made, and the wire tightened up again (See Figure 6.7).

Steel fence posts

These posts are specified in the various parts of BS 1772 on fencing. Mild steel rolled angle posts ('angle irons') and struts are used mainly with chain-link fencing, especially in tennis courts and other sports areas. Intermediate posts are plain angle irons while the straining posts with their struts are supplied ready-drilled for assembly on site and come complete with fixings; the types available include special end posts, intermediate straining posts, internal corner posts, external corner posts and gate posts. All posts can be supplied with straight or cranked extension arms for barbed wire and the gate posts are drilled to accept gate hinges. They should always be set in concrete footings as for timber posts except that no drainage is needed since the angle iron does not expand or contract significantly. Angle irons are usually supplied primed at the works to BS 3698 or 5193 and subsequently painted on site with a metal protective paint, metal-coated at the works, or hot-dip galvanized. Typical sizes and lengths of angle-iron posts are shown in Table 6.4.

Steel angle posts lend themselves very well to the tie-and-brace method of strutting end and corner posts in which two posts are set about 1 m apart with a horizontal brace between their tops and with a diagonal wire tie from the bottom of the end post to the top of the second post. This wire is fixed so that it may be tightened to bring the posts vertical and can be adjusted at any time, either by tightening a turnbuckle in the tie or by using a threaded eye-bolt. This type of fixing does not depend on the support of the ground to keep the posts vertical and is therefore very useful in poor ground or where pressure on the fence is likely to cause sagging from time to time, as might be the case in school playgrounds (See Figure 6.8).

6.2   CONCRETE POST-AND-PANEL FENCES

These fences consist of special reinforced concrete posts with grooves on each side into which precast reinforced concrete panels of varying sizes and finishes are slotted. These fences are used mainly as a more economical substitute for brick or stone walls, and they have the advantage that, being a

Table 6.4
Steel-angle posts

medium posts are:	40 × 40 × 3 mm
heavy posts are:	40 × 40 × 5 mm
extra-heavy posts are:	50 × 50 × 6 mm

1500 mm long with 600 mm in ground gives a 900 mm high fence
1800 mm long with 600 mm in ground gives a 1200 mm high fence
2000 mm long with 600 mm in ground gives a 1400 mm high fence
2600 mm long with 800 mm in ground gives a 1800 mm high fence
3200 mm long with 800 mm in ground gives a 2400 mm high fence
3500 mm long with 750 mm in ground gives a 2750 mm high fence
3800 mm long with 750 mm in ground gives a 3050 mm high fence

dry construction, a damaged panel can easily be replaced. Being solid and made of dense material they can absorb more sound than a timber or wire fence, as the greater the mass of a material the more sound it can absorb (sound attenuation capacity) and are therefore frequently used along motorways and railway yards to reduce noise transmission to adjoining housing, while their sturdy appearance and more or less unclimbable face makes them suitable as a vandal deterrent fence. They are sometimes finished with a vertical board fence mounted on the front to give a better appearance on important contracts, while the softer irregular surface of the boarding prevents sound from being reflected back onto the road or railway. A typical aggregate faced panel is about 300 mm high × 50 mm thick and is designed to slot into grooved posts at 2 m centres. Finishes include plain or coloured concrete, profiled panels and aggregate facing to one or both sides of the panels. The posts are plain precast concrete similar in appearance to ordinary concrete fencing posts, made in a range of lengths, and they may be fitted with precast concrete cranked extension arms to carry barbed wire or tape. Panels are designed to fit the posts accurately so that the posts are best set in concrete footings to ensure accuracy, and it follows that the fence is most economically designed if its length is a multiple of the panel length. Typical sizes of fences are listed in Table 6.5. (See Figure 6.9)

A version of post-and-panel fencing is the 'picket' fence made of concrete pickets cast integrally with their rails to simulate timber picket fencing. Pickets are short pointed pales or posts which were originally used as temporary tethering posts for cavalry in the field or driven into the ground close together to form a stockade, so a fence consisting of these pickets became known as a picket fence. Nowadays timber pickets are assembled onto rails as a panel which is fixed to posts, and the precast concrete simulation is cast in one piece and bolted to short concrete posts set in footings as previously described. These picket fences are usually 1000 to 1500 mm high and are used as ornamental edging to planted areas. There is a temptation to use post-and-panel fences as light retaining walls but they are not designed for such use and should not be placed where earth or site material is likely to be piled against them. Much the same site precautions as those for brick walls should be enforced, as follows:

- Posts and panels must be stacked on clean dry level surfaces.
- Neither posts nor panels should be dropped or thrown since hair cracks may not show up till weathering takes place.
- Posts and panels should be protected from oil, creosote, cement, mud and other pollutants.
- Since post-and-panel fencing is a dry construction, frost precautions are not required for the fence itself, but concrete footings should not be poured in freezing conditions.
- Posts must be correctly centred and panels must not be so loose that they can be removed, or so tight that they are forced into too small a space. It has been known for contractors to knock most of the nibs off the panels to obtain a fit, and this obviously weakens the fence as well as cracking the panels.
- The aggregate face is easily damaged by machinery and the panel erection should be left as late as possible in the contract.

(See also Figure 6.9).

Table 6.5
Concrete post-and-panel fences

125 × 100 mm posts 1565 mm long, 600 mm in ground with 915mm high fence
125 × 100 mm posts 2335 mm long, 760 mm in ground with 1525 mm high fence
150 × 100 mm posts 3250 mm long, 760 mm in ground with 2440 mm high fence
175 × 125 mm posts 4000 mm long, 900 mm in ground with 3050 mm high fence

---

6.3 TIMBER FENCING

Natural softwood and hardwood timber fences may be classified as pale fences with vertical timber pales, rail fences with horizontal rails, board fences with vertical boards on rails, and plank fences with larger boards spanning posts. There are also a number of ornamental fencing panels such as wattle hurdles, woven wood, trellis, waney-edge lapped boarding, and many others ornamental fencing panels, and the range of these types is only limited by the supply of scrap wood which can be converted into light fencing; but most of them are rather lightly constructed, and are therefore more suitable for domestic garden work than for the landscape contract. The sizes of timber pales, rails, posts and cappings given here are average and for very high-class work carefully selected heavier sections would be appropriate. It is sensible to use stock sizes of timber

Plate 17   **Concrete post and panel**   *Precast aggregate faced panels supported by plain concrete posts. This is a dry construction, and damaged panels can easily be replaced. The landscape designer must ensure that the panels are correctly fitted into the grooved posts, and that nibs are not cut off on site to make the panels fit.*

for fence components unless there is a very good reason for using specials, as site or works cutting adds considerably to the cost. Stock sizes of sawn softwood suitable for fencing are detailed in Table 6.6.

Table 6.6
Stock sizes of softwood

19 × 38, 50, 75, 100, 125 mm
25 × 38, 50, 75, 100, 150, 175, 200 mm
38 × 38, 50, 75, 100, 150, 175, 200, 225 mm
50 × 50, 75, 100, 125, 150, 175, 200, 225 mm
75 × 75, 100, 150, 175, 200, 225 mm
100 × 100, 150, 200 mm

Most fencing manufacturers produce satisfactory standard fence components in their own range of sizes, but any timber sizes smaller than those described under the various fence type headings should be regarded with caution. The choice of timber for fencing is important and the landscape designer must decide on his priorities before specifying a particular timber. Initial cost, maintenance costs, appearance, compatibility with the landscape or buildings, vandal resistance, availability of timber stocks, durability in adverse ground or climatic conditions, and ease of working are all factors which must be considered. If money is no object it is possible to use very durable timbers such as teak, jarrah or greenheart, but except for the occasio-

Table 6.7
Timbers suitable for fencing

Name	Natural durability	Treatment	Hardness	Colour
Western red cedar*	15–25 yrs	none	soft	grey
Sweet chestnut	15–25 yrs	none	medium	brown
American oak	15–35 yrs	none	hard	grey/brown
European oak	15–25 yrs	none	hard	grey/brown
Robinia	15–25 yrs	none	hard	yellow/brown
Yew	15–25 yrs	none	tough	yellow
Douglas fir	10–15 yrs	treat	soft	white
Larch	10–15 years	treat	soft	white
Turkey oak	10–15 yrs	treat	medium	brown
Birch	5–10 yrs	treat	soft	white
Dutch elm	5–10 yrs	treat	medium	brown
Fir (most species)	5–10 yrs	treat	soft	white
American red oak	5–10 yrs	treat	medium	reddish
Pine (most species)	5–10 yrs	treat	soft	yellow/white
Grey poplar	5–10 yrs	treat	soft	white
Spruce (most species)	5–10 yrs	treat	soft	white

*British-grown Western red cedar is not so durable

nal very prestigious jobs the most commonly available types of timber suitable for fencing are those listed in Table 6.7.

The estimated life of these timbers naturally depends on the ground conditions and on the way in which the timber was matured and treated, and the figures given in Table 6.7 should be regarded as guidelines only. After the storm of 1987 and also after the lesser storms in later years much local timber such as ash, birch, hornbeam, black poplar, sycamore, horse chestnut, and willow has become available, but these timbers are not naturally durable and depend entirely on preservative treatment so that they are only suitable for temporary protective fencing. Any timber taken from storm-felled trees should be carefully inspected to ensure that it is free from infection and defects, since many of these trees were in poor condition before they fell, and they may also have stress cracks caused by the wind and by ground impact. English elm was traditionally used for posts in wet ground, as the wetter the ground the harder the timber became, but the only stocks now available are from diseased trees, and only sound timber impregnated with preservative should be permitted. Where planting is to be carried out adjacent to timber fencing, only those preservatives which are not inimical to plants should be specified unless the harmful solvents have had time to disperse completely, and the preservative manufacturer should supply information on this point. Timber for fencing is not usually stress-graded in the way required for structural timber, though any timber with severe shakes, waney edges, knots on edges, loose knots, and knots larger than a sixth of the face dimension should be rejected except where the fence is for temporary work only. Some timbers such as elm or oak may have shakes which do not reduce the strength of the timber to any appreciable extent.

Pale fences

Pale fences are usually used for temporary site protection or for rough fencing round gardens or parkland where appearance is less important than cost. Where greater protection is required the pales and the posts should be closer together. The most common form is the cleft chestnut pale fence specified in BS 1722: part 4 which is made from small chestnut saplings grown as stools in a coppice and harvested at seven years old, cleft into three or four pales, and then woven with four stranded 1.9 mm galvanized wire to form a continuous paling fence. Only the 75 mm diameter timber supporting posts are driven into the ground at 2 to 2.5 m centres while the paling is attached to straining posts by eyebolts; the paling should only be pulled tight by hand, not by power tools. Concrete intermediate posts may be at 3 m centres. Although line wires are not usually considered necessary, it is advisable to use a top wire where people or stock are likely to lean on the fence as continual stretching may slacken the fence and loosen the pales. Straining posts should not be further than 45 m apart and should be strutted. Chestnut pale fencing is manufactured in various heights and strengths, as follows:

- *Contractors fencing*: unbarked, unpointed pales 75 mm apart, 1200 mm high with three lines of wire. This is intended for temporary protective fencing only, such as guarding new grass or planting until it is established.
- *Permanent or semi-permanent fencing*: the pales are barked and pointed at the top. Pales may be 50, 75, or 100 mm apart, and obviously the closer the pales the stronger the fence, and the more animal proof. Fences with two lines of wire are 750, 900, 1100, and 1200 mm high. Higher fences

with three lines of wire are 900, 1100, 1200, 1400, 1500, 1750, and 1800 mm high. (See Figure 6.10).

- *'Spile' fencing*, which has cleft chestnut spiles similar to pales but about 50 mm diameter each driven into the ground at 150 mm centres and secured with two or three rows of 4 mm seven-ply line wire according to height. Fence posts similar to those used for chestnut pale fencing are used at 3 m intervals to stiffen the fence. This is more rigid than pale fencing as each spile is driven into the ground.

Palisade and picket fences

The picket fence consists of light dressed timber pales with tops of various profiles (usually softwood painted) nailed to horizontal rails which are in turn fixed to supporting posts. The pales are usually 75 × 19 mm or 25 mm softwood treated with preservative or painted, with flat bottoms and sharply pointed tops, spaced 15 to 20 mm apart and (in good class work) screwed to the rails which are 89 × 38 mm bolted to 100 × 100 square posts at 2.5 m centres. Two or three rails may be used according to the height of the fence and the most common heights are 900, 1000, and 1200 mm. These fences are traditionally associated with cottage gardens, but nowadays they are used decoratively around planted areas, though they should not be used round playgrounds because of the danger of impalement. The term 'palisade' is used for higher versions of the picket fence and is covered by BS 1722:part 6:1986. It is intended as a more serious obstacle 1050, 1200, 1500, 1650 and 1800 mm high and may have extension arms on the higher fences for barbed wire. The pales are 75 × 20mm at 75mm centres or 65 × 20mm at 65 mm centres with two or three rails 89 × 38 mm on 100 × 100 mm or 100 × 125 mm posts at 3 m centres. A stronger 1800 mm fence may be erected on 100 × 150 mm posts at 2 m centres (See Figure 6.11).

Post and rail fences

Rail, or post-and-rail, fences are most suited to countryside projects since they blend well into all landscapes (except stone-wall country) and are proof against large stock and vehicles. They can easily be climbed without being damaged or causing injury to walkers and can be jumped by horsemen. They can be constructed and erected by volunteer labour since local light timber can be used for both posts and rails, which makes them popular with country landlords and amenity organizations.

The simplest and least expensive type consists of three 100 mm diameter half round treated softwood rails (usually young plantation thinnings) nailed with 100 mm galvanized wire nails to 100 mm round or half-round posts 1700 or 1800 mm long, driven 600 mm into the ground at 2 m centres. No straining posts are required since there is no tension on the rails. The fence may be treated with plain or coloured timber preservative, creosoted, or painted with solid colour wood stain (See Figure 6.12).

127

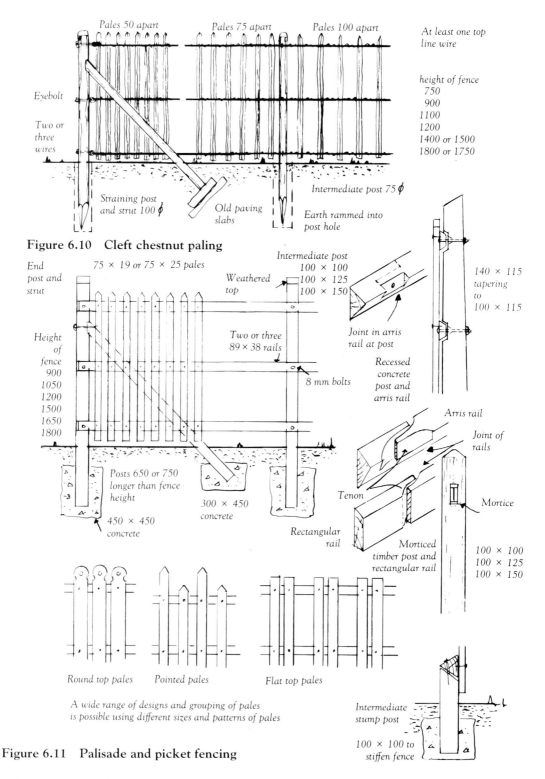

Pales 50 apart   Pales 75 apart   Pales 100 apart

At least one top
line wire

Eyebolt

Two or
three
wires

height of fence
750
900
1100
1200
1400 or 1500
1800 or 1750

Straining post
and strut 100 ⌀

Old paving
slabs

Intermediate post 75 ⌀

Earth rammed into
post hole

Figure 6.10   Cleft chestnut paling

End
post and
strut

75 × 19 or 75 × 25 pales

Intermediate post
100 × 100
100 × 125
100 × 150

Weathered
top

140 × 115
tapering
to
100 × 115

Height
of
fence
900
1050
1200
1500
1650
1800

Two or three
89 × 38 rails

8 mm bolts

Joint in arris
rail at post

Recessed
concrete
post and
arris rail

Arris rail

Joint of
rails

Posts 650 or 750
longer than fence
height

300 × 450
concrete

450 × 450
concrete

Rectangular
rail

Tenon

Mortice

Morticed
timber post and
rectangular rail

100 × 100
100 × 125
100 × 150

Round top pales   Pointed pales   Flat top pales

A wide range of designs and grouping of pales
is possible using different sizes and patterns of pales

Intermediate
stump post

100 × 100 to
stiffen fence

Figure 6.11   Palisade and picket fencing

128

Plate 18   Picket fence   *A low picket fence used to protect a garden. A higher palisade fence would allow a glimpse of the garden to be seen between the palisades. White paint emphasizes the fence; dark woodstain would blend it into the background. The gate can be a standard four or five bar gate, or can be made with pickets to match the fence.*

Dressed post and rail

A slightly more expensive type, it is similar to the plain post-and-rail except that both rails and posts are squared off, giving a neater but less rural appearance more suited to semi-urban situations such as parks and recreation areas. The fence is constructed of three 100 × 38 mm treated softwood rails, nailed to 100 × 100 or 125 × 75 mm posts 1800 or 2100 mm long with their tops weathered to shed rain. These fences are sometimes specified with the rails housed or half-housed into the posts, where the rails are set into a notch cut in the post which is either the whole or half the thickness of the rail. This makes the rails less likely to pull out from their nails when the weight of a climber is put on them, although the housing does provide a lodging for water and algae which may eventually rot the post or the rail. In any case the housing should never exceed a quarter of the post thickness (See Figure 6.13).

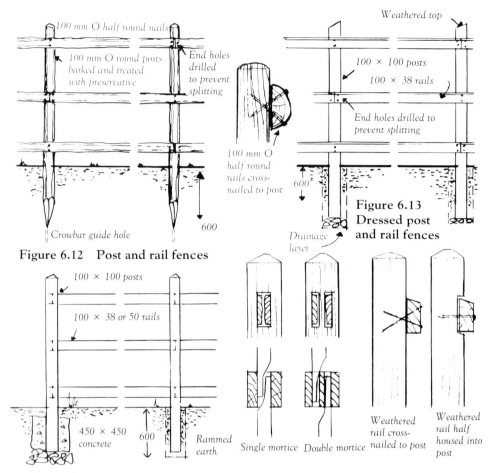

100 mm O half round nails

100 mm O round posts barked and treated with preservative

End holes drilled to prevent splitting

100 mm O half round rails cross-nailed to post

Crowbar guide hole

600

Figure 6.12   Post and rail fences

Weathered top

100 × 100 posts

100 × 38 rails

End holes drilled to prevent splitting

600

Drainage layer

**Figure 6.13
Dressed post
and rail fences**

100 × 100 posts

100 × 38 or 50 rails

450 × 450 concrete

600

Rammed earth

Drainage layer

Single mortice

Double mortice

Weathered rail cross-nailed to post

Weathered rail half housed into post

Figure 6.14   Morticed post and rail fences

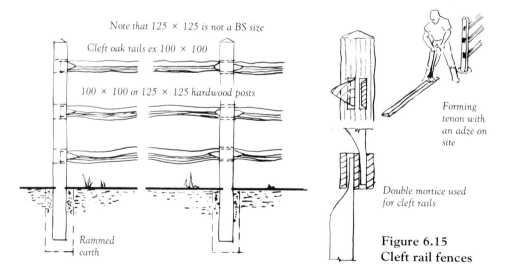

Note that 125 × 125 is not a BS size

Cleft oak rails ex 100 × 100

100 × 100 or 125 × 125 hardwood posts

Rammed earth

Forming tenon with an adze on site

Double mortice used for cleft rails

**Figure 6.15
Cleft rail fences**

Morticed post and rail

A sturdier and more durable type of post-and-rail fence is of nail-free construction with the rails tenoned (tapered off to fit the mortice) into the posts. A mortice is cut in the post and the end of the rail is tenoned and set (not driven) into this mortice. This method is naturally more expensive than the plain post-and-rail fence but does not suffer from 'nail sickness', and the rails can only be removed by breaking or cutting them. It is obvious that the fence has to be erected as a single entity and that the rails cannot be removed for the passage of contractors' vehicles, so it is therefore advisable to specify gates wide enough to take the largest contractors' or agricultural plant likely to use the site – ploughing engines and combine harvesters should be borne in mind. The tapered ends of the rails are set either side by side in one mortice or, preferably, in two separate mortices in the post, and it is important that the landscape designer does not allow the rails to be driven hard into the post as swelling would split the mortice. The sizes of rails and posts are as for nailed fences, but intermediate dropper posts are sometimes used to increase the distance between posts. The rails are sometimes nailed through the tenons but this defeats the object of a nail-free fence and rusting of the nails may split the tenon (See Figure 6.14).

Cleft rail fence

The most durable and aesthetically satisfying of all the rail fences is the riven oak fence, whose rails are made of cleft oak, barked or unbarked, and tenoned at each end to fit into morticed posts. This is a high-class fence often used for prosperous country estates or country parks where durability and appearance are more important than cost. The rails are naturally irregular in shape and although this adds to their appearance, they should not be so uneven as to leave over-wide gaps between the rails. The cleft rail is roughly triangular with 100 mm faces, set arris (corner) uppermost with the flat side against the post, and each rail is set into a separate mortice. The length is variable, but on average rails are 2.5 to 3 m long. The posts are usually hardwood, natural round or squared chestnut or oak, although treated softwood 100 × 100 mm may be used (See Figure 6.15).

Close boarded fence

Close-boarded fencing is covered by BS 1722: Part 5 which deals with the boards, rails, posts and fixings. Board fencing (close-boarded or featherboarded fencing) is most suitable for residential fences where privacy is important and where vandalism or casual damage is not likely to occur. They cast a solid shade which will affect the choice of adjacent planting, and can easily be distorted or even split if climbers are allowed to penetrate the slight gaps between the boards. As the storms in recent years have shown, they are vulnerable to strong winds and should not be used in exposed situations where a hit-and-miss fence as described below would be more suitable.

131

Plate 19 Cleft rail fence   *An expensive but very durable fence. The rails cannot be removed without destroying the fence, so a gate should be provided for machinery or emergency access. The traditional fence is made of matured English oak, but unless storm damaged timber is available, treated softwood may have to be used for the posts, though the rails should always be hardwood.*

The fence is constructed either by fixing boards to rails and posts on site, or by fixing pre-fabricated panels of boarding and rails to posts on site. Panels are more economical for straight runs which are multiples of the panel size since they can be mass-produced, but individual boards are more suited to uneven ground and irregular lengths. Each board is 100 mm wide and tapers across its width from about 13 to 6 mm (feathered) and they are nailed to the rails with 75 mm galvanized nails at the rate of 12 per metre, with an overlap of about 18 mm. They are traditionally oak but cheaper types may be treated softwood. The rails are either rectangular section 75 × 38 mm or 100 × 100 mm, or what is called 'arris' rails, which is triangular in section with a flat side against the boards made from 75 × 75 mm or 87 × 87 mm timber. These rails may be set on recessed concrete posts so that their face is flush with the posts, enabling the boarding to be carried straight across the post. Standard fence heights are 1050 and 1200 mm with two rails and 1500, 1650, and 1800 mm with three rails. In order to give a more finished appearance to the fence, a hardwood capping (usually oak) 65 × 38 mm is sometimes added.

At the foot of the fence is fixed a timber gravel board 150 × 25 or 32 mm whose function is to save the bottoms of the feather boards from damp, to take impact from tools and machinery, and to prevent gravel or earth drifting under the fence. Concrete gravel boards 150 × 50 mm are available and are less prone to rot. Care must be taken to ensure that earth is not allowed to pile up above the gravel board at the base of the fence and cause rotting. Gravel boards are meant to be renewed several times in the life of a fence since without them the renewal of numerous rotted boards would mean the practical reconstruction of the fence.

Timber posts at 3 m centres are treated softwood 100 × 100 or 125 mm or oak 100 × 100 mm, weathered on top, morticed at the works and set 750 m into the ground in concrete footings as described above in the section on posts for wire fences. End, gate, and corner posts should be 125 × 125 mm. Metposts as previously described may be used for timber posts if there is inadequate access or if constructing concrete footings is not practicable, though the larger timbers will have to be rebated to fit the sockets. Alternatively, precast concrete posts as specified in the British Standard with slots for the rail tenons or recesses on the face for the rails may be used, set in concrete footings, and although these do not look so homogeneous as timber posts they are less likely to suffer from rot caused by earthing up (See Figure 6.16).

British Standard references for close-boarded fences indicate: the material (P = oak, B = other timber); the post type (C = concrete, R = recessed, M = morticed, W = oak); the height in centrimetres: so that PCR105 means an oak pale fence 1050 mm high with recessed concrete posts. Concrete posts are either straight morticed posts 140 × 115 mm, or tapered recessed posts 140 × 115 mm to 100 × 115 mm. (See Figure 6.16 and Plates 20 and 21)

Table 6.8
British Standard close-boarded fences

Situation	No. of rails	Size of timber post	BS reference
Gardens	2	100 × 100 mm	???105
Housing fences, gardens	2	100 × 100 mm	???120
Housing fences, gardens	3	100 × 100 mm	???150
General visual privacy, parks	3	100 × 100 mm	???165
Screening, patios, parks, schools	3	100 × 100 mm	???180A
Commercial light security	3	100 × 150 mm	???180B

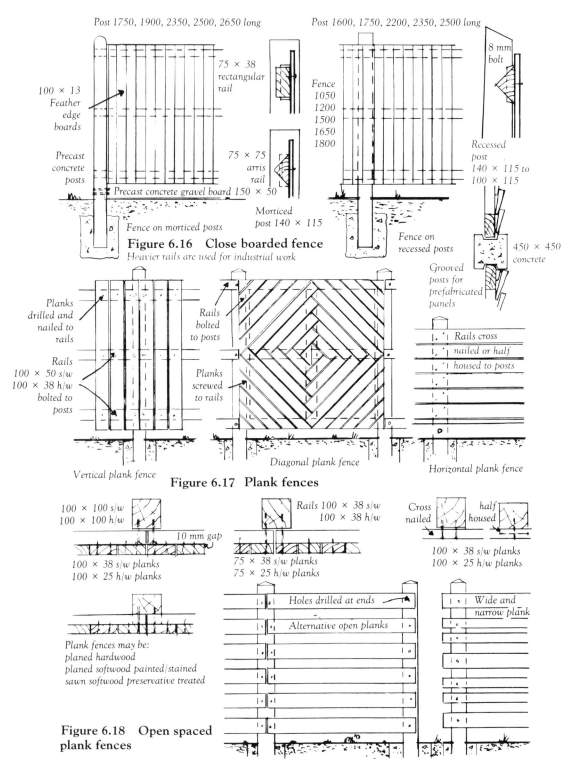

Post 1750, 1900, 2350, 2500, 2650 long

Post 1600, 1750, 2200, 2350, 2500 long

100 × 13
Feather
edge
boards

75 × 38
rectangular
rail

8 mm
bolt

Precast
concrete
posts

75 × 75
arris
rail

Fence
1050
1200
1500
1650
1800

Recessed
post
140 × 115 to
100 × 115

Precast concrete gravel board 150 × 50

Fence on morticed posts

Morticed
post 140 × 115

Fence on
recessed posts

Grooved
posts for
prefabricated
panels

450 × 450
concrete

Figure 6.16   Close boarded fence
Heavier rails are used for industrial work

Planks
drilled and
nailed to
rails

Rails
bolted
to posts

Rails cross
nailed or half
housed to posts

Rails
100 × 50 s/w
100 × 38 h/w
bolted to
posts

Planks
screwed
to rails

Vertical plank fence

Diagonal plank fence

Horizontal plank fence

Figure 6.17   Plank fences

100 × 100 s/w
100 × 100 h/w

Rails 100 × 38 s/w
100 × 38 h/w

Cross
nailed

half
housed

10 mm gap

100 × 38 s/w planks
100 × 25 h/w planks

75 × 38 s/w planks
75 × 25 h/w planks

100 × 38 s/w planks
100 × 25 h/w planks

Plank fences may be:
planed hardwood
planed softwood painted/stained
sawn softwood preservative treated

Holes drilled at ends

Alternative open planks

Wide and
narrow plank

**Figure 6.18   Open spaced
plank fences**

Plate 20   Close boarded fence   *The front of the fence shows a smooth surface. The posts may be concealed behind the boarding, or left showing as in the photograph. Timber or precast concrete posts may be used, and a concrete or timber gravel board should be fixed to prevent the bottom of the feather boards from rotting. Although not so attractive, a concrete gravel board is more practical if earth is likely to be piled against the fence.*

Plank fences

Plank fences consist of boards fixed to posts in a variety of patterns such as open-spaced, hit-and-miss, diagonal, and any other patterns suggested by the ingenuity of the landscape designer. They are best suited to residential and light public space use where vandalism is not serious, but where a certain amount of privacy and restricted access is necessary and a sturdier fence than the close-boarded type is desirable. They can be treated with coloured preservative stain for an informal effect or painted white for more urban situations as the landscape designer chooses, and brown posts with white planks can look very smart. Boarded or planked fences can be designed in many patterns, diagonal boards, vertical boards, diamond pattern, or even perforated boards, and almost any pattern can be constructed on site, though the cost will increase with the amount of cutting and waste timber involved. Solid

135

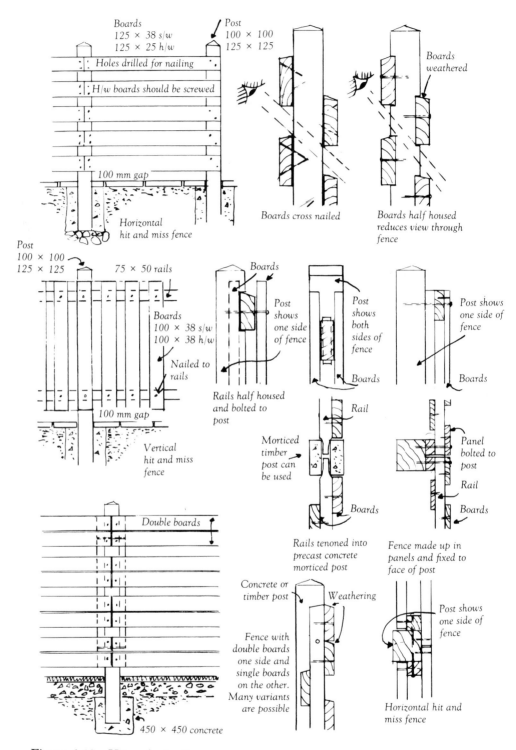

Figure 6.19   Hit and miss fences

136

Plate 21   Close boarded fence   *The rear view of the close boarded fence, showing the arris rails tenoned into the concrete post. As this fence is on a public road close to a school, an intermediate post has been fitted here to srengthen the fence.*

board fences are vulnerable to strong winds and should only be erected where there is little risk of wind damage (See Figure 6.17 and Table 6.8).

Open-spaced plank fences

Open-spaced plank fences are robust in appearance and are made up on site from boards of various sizes nailed, or preferably bolted, to timber posts. A typical light plank fence construction would be 75 × 75 mm softwood posts at 2 m centres in Metposts or concrete footings, with eight 125 × 19 mm softwood boards set 25 mm apart which would make a fence 1225 mm high, including a 50 mm space at the bottom to keep the fence away from ground damp. A larger scale fence would be constructed of 100 × 100 mm posts at 2 m centres with ten 150 × 25 mm boards and 50 mm gaps between boards,

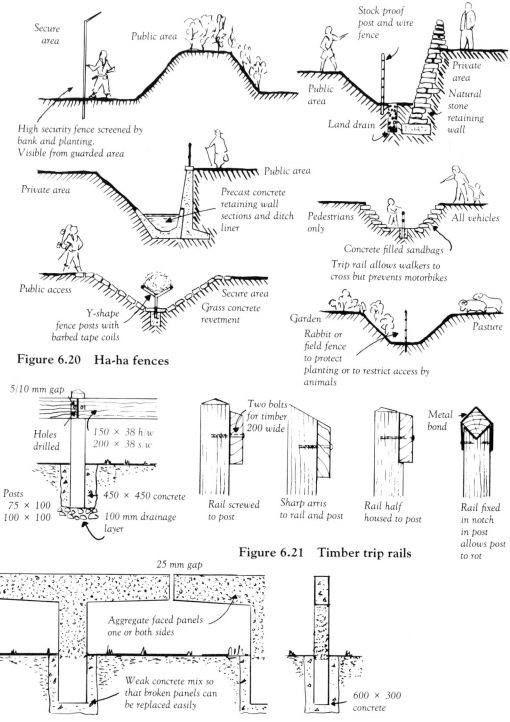

Secure area

Public area

High security fence screened by
bank and planting.
Visible from guarded area

Stock proof
post and wire
fence

Public
area

Land drain

Private
area

Natural
stone
retaining
wall

Private area

Public area

Precast concrete
retaining wall
sections and ditch
liner

Pedestrians
only

All vehicles

Concrete filled sandbags

Trip rail allows walkers to
cross but prevents motorbikes

Public access

Y-shape
fence posts with
barbed tape coils

Secure area
Grass concrete
revetment

Garden

Rabbit or
field fence
to protect
planting or to restrict access by
animals

Pasture

Figure 6.20   Ha-ha fences

5/10 mm gap

Holes
drilled

150 × 38 h/w
200 × 38 s/w

Posts
75 × 100
100 × 100

450 × 450 concrete

100 mm drainage
layer

Two bolts
for timber
200 wide

Rail screwed
to post

Sharp arris
to rail and post

Rail half
housed to post

Metal
bond

Rail fixed
in notch
in post
allows post
to rot

Figure 6.21   Timber trip rails

25 mm gap

Aggregate faced panels
one or both sides

Weak concrete mix so
that broken panels can
be replaced easily

600 × 300
concrete

Figure 6.22   Precast concrete trip rails

which would give a fence 2000 mm high. These fences provide a good barrier without being totally obstructive to the view or liable to blow down in high winds, although they can be climbed without difficulty (See Figure 6.18).

Hit-and miss fences

Hit-and-miss fences are still open-spaced, but the boards are staggered on each face of the posts, so that although wind can pass through the fence it is difficult to obtain more than a narrow slot view through it. This type is more suitable where greater privacy is needed and is often specified as a division between terrace house gardens immediately adjacent to the building. Boards and posts of the sizes described above are equally suitable for a hit-and-miss fence, but since the boards must overlap by 25mm on alternate sides to give privacy, more boards are required to produce the same height of fence. For example, twelve 125 mm boards would be required to make a fence 1275 mm high including the 50 mm gap at ground level. A variant on the horizontal hit-and-miss fence is the vertical hit-and-miss fence which is constructed with panels of 100×25 mm or 150×25 mm vertical boards staggered on opposite sides of 75×50 mm top and bottom rails. The boards should be screwed to the rails and the rails should be bolted to 100×38 mm or 150×38 mm side framing, and the complete panel bolted to 125×75mm timber posts or concrete posts at 2 m centres (See Figure 6.19).

6.4 HA-HA FENCES

A variant on the standard fence is the ha-ha or sunk fence. This fence offers good stock protection without any obstruction to the view, and can if necessary be constructed to deter trespassers. It is an ideal fence for country parks where an attractive landscape can be viewed without any visual barrier. The ha-ha is constructed by excavating a ditch as deep as the fence is high, and setting the fence in the bottom of this ditch so that from a distance no barrier is visible. Alternatively one side of the ditch may be a retaining wall, and if a higher barrier is necessary the retaining wall may be surmounted by a low fence so that the wall and fence combined are the desired height and all that will be apparent is the low fence. Since the bottom of the ditch is likely to collect water, it should be drained and only damp resistant posts and fencing used. Field fencing or plain line wires on timber posts provide minimum stock control and additional security or strength can be obtained by using cast iron or tubular steel stanchions with tubular steel rails, concrete posts with chain-link fencing, or concrete posts with welded-mesh security fencing as described below (See Figure 6.20).

Plate 22   Open spaced plank fence   *A simple screen fence round a small garden. It is possible to peer through this fence if the public path runs close to it, so that hit and miss fences, which provide greater privacy, should be used in more public areas.*

6.5   TRIP RAILS

These are low rails whose name explains itself, but the landscape designer is advised to make sure that no one can actually trip over the rail. Their function is to deter pedestrians and vehicles from crossing grassed or planted areas, but they offer little obstruction to active trainer-wearers who can jog quite happily over them. They are probably most effective as vehicle and cycle barriers around village greens and open grass areas in business parks, country parks, and recreation areas since they offer little visual obstruction and may be painted white or stained dark depending on whether they are required to be conspicuous or not. They may be made of timber, concrete, or steel tubing, and PVC U versions are available though these are more suitable for domestic gardens as they are rather too fragile for public use.

Timber trip rails

Timber trip rails should be not less than 400 mm high and a suitable specifica-tion would be 200 × 38 mm treated softwood rails bolted to 100 × 100 mm treated softwood posts 1000 mm long, set in concrete footings at 1.5 m centres and fixed with two 8 mm coach bolts or screws per rail. The top surface of both rails and posts should be weathered, and a 5 mm gap should be left between the ends of the rails to allow for expansion. The trip rails may be stained or painted white, and if oak or red cedar are used in place of softwood they do not require any treatment. A lighter rail for residential use would be 150 × 38 mm rails on 75 × 100 mm posts. An alternative type of rail is sometimes seen where a square hardwood rail is set on its arris into a vee notch in the top of the post, being held in place by galvanized steel bands bolted to the posts; but this fence suffers from the collection of rain in the base of the notch which may eventually rot the post, and although the design does prevent people from balancing or sitting on it, the construction is not satisfactory (See Figure 6.21).

Precast concrete trip rails

Precast concrete trip rails are supplied complete by specialist firms of precast concrete manufacturers and they are usually an aggregate-faced composite unit comprising a post and rail which are set into the ground with the rail ends nearly touching (See Figure 6.22).

Metal trip rails

Metal trip rails are most often made of galvanized tubular steel rails, either jointed and socketed to tubular steel posts with ordinary tubular railing joints, or passed through a preformed hole in 100 × 100 mm oak or 250 mm diameter concrete barrel posts. Rails made of steel angles can cause injury if anyone trips over them, and are best avoided. A suitable specification would be 38 mm internal diameter mild steel tubes rails connected with sleeved joints, and 38 mm internal diameter posts at 1500 mm centres set into concrete footings. Square hollow section tubes 38 mm square with joints welded on site may be used instead, but they are more expensive and the improved appearance may not justify the cost. Metal trip rails should be galvanized, and may be painted or left self-colour where wear is likely to be heavy since patchy paint looks worse than plain galvanizing. A useful version of the metal trip rail is the Y-rail which has two rails on a Y-shaped post with the arms about 900 mm apart. This is much more difficult to jump over than the single rail and is constructed of 60 mm diameter prefabricated tubular steel posts set in concrete footings with 30 mm diameter tubular steel rails 900 mm above ground (See Figure 6.23).

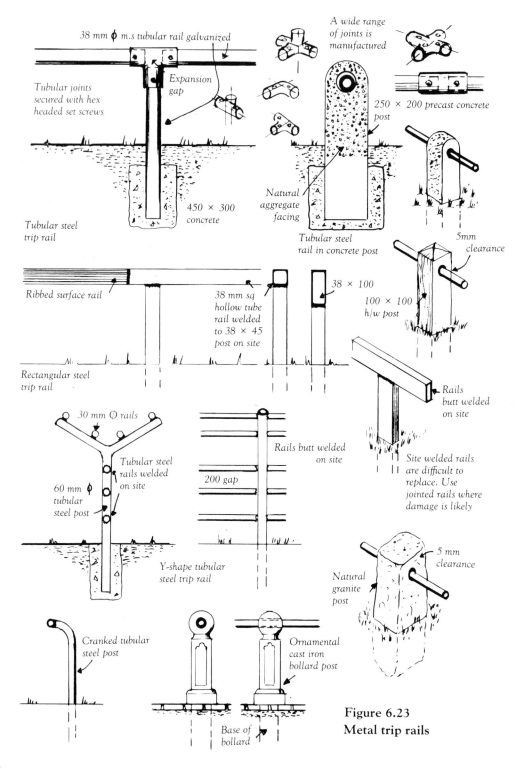

38 mm φ m.s tubular rail galvanized

A wide range of joints is manufactured

Tubular joints secured with hex headed set screws

Expansion gap

250 × 200 precast concrete post

450 × 300 concrete

Tubular steel trip rail

Natural aggregate facing

Tubular steel rail in concrete post

5mm clearance

Ribbed surface rail

38 mm sq hollow tube rail welded to 38 × 45 post on site

38 × 100

100 × 100 h/w post

Rectangular steel trip rail

Rails butt welded on site

30 mm ⌀ rails

Tubular steel rails welded on site

60 mm φ tubular steel post

Rails butt welded on site

200 gap

Site welded rails are difficult to replace. Use jointed rails where damage is likely

Y-shape tubular steel trip rail

Cranked tubular steel post

Ornamental cast iron bollard post

Natural granite post

5 mm clearance

Base of bollard

Figure 6.23 Metal trip rails

6.6   PLAYGROUND FENCING

Any of the previously described types of fencing may be used for fences around playgrounds, provided that certain criteria are met, as follows:

- The fence must have no spikes, sharp edges or arrises where children can cut or impale themselves.
- It must either be unclimbable or so low that children cannot fall off and break or sprain limbs.
- It must not be liable to produce splinters or jagged edges whether accidentally or intentionally produced.
- There must be no projecting fastenings to catch flesh or clothes and all bolt heads and nuts should be sunk and preferably removable only with special tools.
- Gates should not swing or slam so as to trap fingers or toes against posts and walls or between pairs of gates and they should not open across public footways or footpaths. Kissing gates provide a safe egress from playgrounds, but if prams, bicycles and vehicles must have access, gates should be made to open inwards only and to be rapidly self-closing (though not slamming), with a barrier placed athwart the gateway to prevent children from running straight out.
- All gaps between wires, boards or rails should be no more than 100 mm to prevent heads from getting trapped.
- Any playground boundary fence giving onto trafficked roads should be unclimbable and should have a mesh which will stop small balls such as golf or squash balls, though it is not possible to prevent smaller projectiles the size of marbles being thrown through unless a solid wall is provided.
- Paint or preservative should be non-toxic, non-peelable and non-staining.
- If, for cost reasons, light mesh or chain-link perimeter fencing has to be used, the client should be made aware that regular inspection and maintenance will be required, as light wire fences are very easily vandalized and may then cause injury to children.
- Any accident to children in a playground is always the subject of a thorough inquiry, and being an emotive subject it inevitably gets into the news. The landscape designer should therefore be particularly careful when specifying playground fencing.

6.7   SECURITY FENCING

Security fences are increasingly being installed as part of the contract for industrial and public building contracts, and even private estates are finding it necessary to have media- and tourist-proof fencing. The more serious type of security required by terrorist targets is highly specialized and is outside the

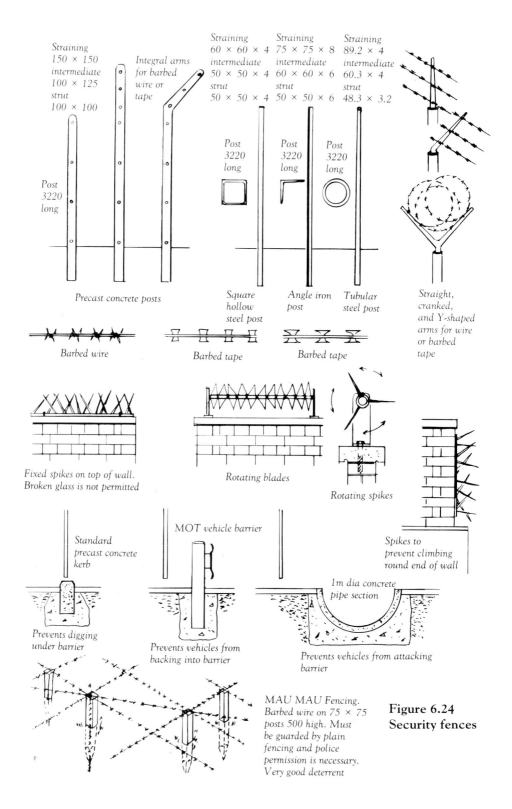

Straining
150 × 150
intermediate
100 × 125
strut
100 × 100

Post
3220
long

Integral arms
for barbed
wire or
tape

Precast concrete posts

Straining
60 × 60 × 4
intermediate
50 × 50 × 4
strut
50 × 50 × 4

Post
3220
long

Square
hollow
steel post

Straining
75 × 75 × 8
intermediate
60 × 60 × 6
strut
50 × 50 × 6

Post
3220
long

Angle iron
post

Straining
89.2 × 4
intermediate
60.3 × 4
strut
48.3 × 3.2

Post
3220
long

Tubular
steel post

Straight,
cranked,
and Y-shaped
arms for wire
or barbed
tape

Barbed wire

Barbed tape

Barbed tape

Fixed spikes on top of wall.
Broken glass is not permitted

Rotating blades

Rotating spikes

Spikes to
prevent climbing
round end of wall

Standard
precast concrete
kerb

Prevents digging
under barrier

MOT vehicle barrier

Prevents vehicles from
backing into barrier

1m dia concrete
pipe section

Prevents vehicles from attacking
barrier

MAU MAU Fencing.
Barbed wire on 75 × 75
posts 500 high. Must
be guarded by plain
fencing and police
permission is necessary.
Very good deterrent

**Figure 6.24
Security fences**

144

scope of this book since it relies more on sophisticated electronic detection than on physical barriers. The landscape designer does not usually design a security fence himself as they are marketed as special systems by the fencing manufacturers, but it may be useful to describe the most common types. Manufacturers usually offer gates to match the fencing, and the gate furniture is supplied complete, so that it is necessary to confirm locking requirements with the client and his insurance company before ordering the gates, and to check with the emergency services that they can get access if necessary. Security fences are either wire mesh or palisade construction. Useful advice on security precautions in general, including fencing, may be found in BS 8220:Pt 3:1990; although this has been written for industrial purposes, the information is relevant to any security problem.

Points to bear in mind when designing security fencing and its gates are as follows:

- A narrow mesh should be used that does not allow foothold.
- Barbed or jagged top should be specified to prevent climbing over, and if barbed wire is used droppers must be fitted to prevent the wires from being bunched together.
- Mesh should be buried or set on a concrete sill at least 125 mm wide × 150 mm deep to prevent digging.
- Fencing should only change direction with obtuse angles to prevent 'chimney' climbing.
- No signs, street furniture, trees or other aids to climbing should be on or near the fence, and no vehicles should be allowed near it. If necessary, vehicle barriers may have to be used to keep vehicles away, or a light fence may be placed 1m away from the security fence to prevent anything from being placed against it. Jones and Son may be proud of their splendid logo on the fence, but it is a perfect foothold for intruders.
- Night lighting may be required and electronic security systems need a clear view the length of the fence.
- All fastenings should be hammered over or have clutch heads to prevent unfastening.
- While it is tempting to hide an ugly security fence with shrubs or trees, no planting should be placed near the fence where it might conceal intruders or interrupt electronic systems.
- If serious attack by vehicle ramming or theft of loaded vehicles is likely, a ditch 1000 mm wide × 900 mm deep inside the fence will trap any vehicle's wheels; this can also be used for surface water drainage (See also Figure 6.24).

Wire security fences

The simplest wire fence which gives protection against casual intruders is a 1800 mm or 2000 mm chain-link fence on concrete or steel posts with straight

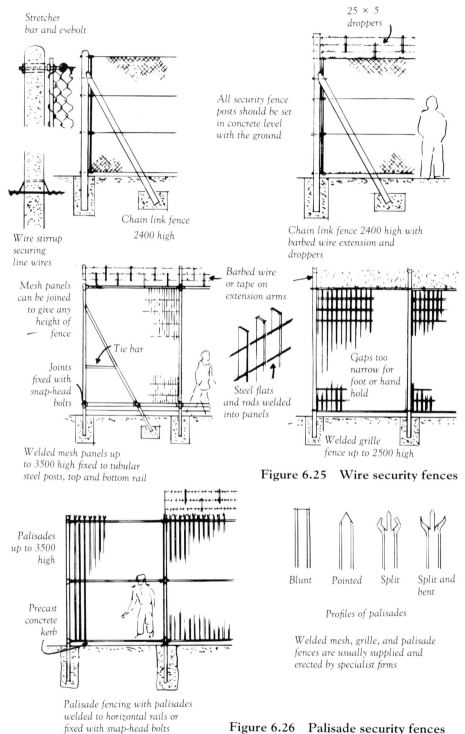

Stretcher bar and eyebolt

Wire stirrup securing line wires

Chain link fence 2400 high

All security fence posts should be set in concrete level with the ground

25 × 5 droppers

Chain link fence 2400 high with barbed wire extension and droppers

Mesh panels can be joined to give any height of fence

Tie bar

Joints fixed with snap-head bolts

Welded mesh panels up to 3500 high fixed to tubular steel posts, top and bottom rail

Barbed wire or tape on extension arms

Steel flats and rods welded into panels

Gaps too narrow for foot or hand hold

Welded grille fence up to 2500 high

Figure 6.25   Wire security fences

Palisades up to 3500 high

Precast concrete kerb

Palisade fencing with palisades welded to horizontal rails or fixed with snap-head bolts

Blunt   Pointed   Split   Split and bent

Profiles of palisades

Welded mesh, grille, and palisade fences are usually supplied and erected by specialist firms

Figure 6.26   Palisade security fences

or cranked arms carrying two or three lines of two-strand galvanized barbed wire. These 'anti-intruder' fences are described in BS 1722 Pt 10. This fence can be penetrated by cutting a flap in the chain-link with heavy wire cutters, and greater security is provided by welded mesh. These fences are supported on intermediate posts of 60.3 mm tubular steel, 50 × 50 mm square hollow section, or 60 × 60 mm rolled steel angles, with straining posts of 89.2 mm galvanized steel tubular posts, 60 × 60 mm rectangular hollow tube posts, or 75 × 75 mm rolled steel angles, and three or four line wires with either heavy or extra heavy chain-link or welded steel mesh attached. Cranked or straight arms carrying barbed wire are fitted if required, giving overall heights of 2000, 2400, 2800 and 3100 mm.

In situations where security is very important, barbed wire or the much more vicious barbed tape may be used (which looks like closely spaced razor blades along a flat steel tape and can cause serious injury), but it must not be fixed lower than 1800 mm above ground where the public have access and must not project over a public path. It is advisable to ensure that barbed tape is clearly visible to persons approaching it, and that warning notices 'DANGER THIS PROPERTY IS PROTECTED BY BARBED TAPE' are visible at all times (which means providing night lighting) since claims for damages may result if anyone inadvertently injures themselves.

High tensile steel wire, which is not vulnerable to ordinary wire cutters, is also manufactured for security fences and is made up into panels of various shapes and patterns which are practically unclimbable. As each manufacturer produces his own patterns, the range is considerable (See Figure 6.25).

Palisade security fences

More serious security fences are palisade fences covered by BS 1722: Part 12:1990 which are classified as General Purpose (GP) fences up to 2400 mm high, and Special Purpose (SP) fences 2400, 3000, and 3600 mm high to deter more intrepid intruders. They are made of mild steel angles or special profile pales welded to horizontal rails at top and bottom which are then secured to posts with inaccessible fastenings, and with their tops split, sharpened and bent outward to form a vee. Most palisade fences are made by specialist fencing firms who supply the fence, gates and fitting complete.

A variation of this type is the slatted fence with vertical steel flats at 65 mm centres welded to horizontal rails 150 mm apart, made up in panels and irremovably fixed to the posts. The slats may be set at an angle to the line of the fence in order to baffle vehicle headlights or to prevent drivers from seeing through the fence while moving.

Where intruders are more persistent some type of spiked guard is fitted to the top rail; these may be rotating spikes or blades, fixed spikes 40 mm long pointing in several directions, lines of barbed tape on extension arms, or one, two or three coils of loosely coiled springy barbed tape wired to the top rail, and this latter is particularly difficult to penetrate since even if it can be cut the coils retain their ability to clutch the intruder. These guards must not be fixed where they can inadvertently injure people, since they are intended to be a serious deterrent and may damage anyone falling or pushing against them and a notice warning the public should be displayed as described in the previous section. The gates for security fences are of similar construction with heavy posts from 152 × 152 mm to 203 × 203 mm according to width, and they must be secured by bars passing through the gate stiles, not surface mounted (See Figure 6.26).

Palisade security fences to BS 1722:Pt 12:1990 are made of corrugated steel pales at least 3 mm thick, welded, bolted or riveted to two horizontal rails fixed to posts at not more than 2750 mm centres (See Table 6.9).

Plate 23   Palisade fence   *This photograph shows a typical medium security entrance to commercial or business premises. The gate is a pole barrier with drop skirt, operated by a control card, and supplemented by heavy braced palisade gates with padlocked bars, hung on steel posts. The palisade fence is galvanized steel painted black to reduce visual impact, and the screen wall is protected by cast iron bollards. This type of protection will not deter serious criminals, but is adequate to prevent casual illegal entry.*

Table 6.9
British Standard palisade security fences

Height	Size of rails	Size of posts	BS reference
2400 mm	45 × 45 × 6 mm	102 × 44 mm RSJ	SP24
3000 mm	50 × 50 × 6 mm	127 × 76 mm UB	SP30
3600 mm	65 × 50 × 6 mm	127 × 76 mm UB	SP36

RSJ is a British Standard rolled steel joist section
UB is a British Standard universal beam section

7 GATES

Landscape designers do not always pay sufficient attention to the design of gates and their appearance, function, construction and furniture are often only superficially specified. The gate to any open or enclosed space is the most important feature of the enclosure as it may convey welcome, security, or privacy; it may allow a view or be uncompromisingly solid. The design of the gate tells the visitor whether he is to enter at will or by permission only, and whether or not he can bring his car, family or dogs in as well. Gates may have to carry coats of arms, logos, notices, warning signs, and other informative material, so these should be designed into the gate from the beginning, since nothing looks worse than a gate or gateposts with scruffy notices and signs added at random. Gates are naturally the hardest worked part of an enclosure, and their 'furniture', (that is, all the fittings which serve to open, close and secure the gate) must be capable of standing up to the intended usage, for example, a pedestrian gate to a public park may be open and shut one-and-a-half million times in a twenty-year life, and some Victorian gates 150 years old are still functioning perfectly. Gates may be made of timber, steel tubing or framed wire mesh and are either specified as part of the fencing contract or as separate items. The specially designed one-off wrought iron gate is outside the scope of this book since such gates are usually produced by master blacksmiths who prepare their own design in consultation with the landscape designer. Gates are ordered as right- or left-handed; a right-handed gate has the hinges on the right-hand side facing the gate when it opens away, with the heads of the bolts showing, while a left-handed gate is the reverse.

7.1 TIMBER AND STEEL GATES

Timber gates are usually specified individually to suit the style of fence chosen. The utilitarian types are known as 'field gates' or 'five-barred gates' while the more finished types are called 'drive' or 'entrance' gates. The main difference is in the selection of the timber and its finish and the field gate

151

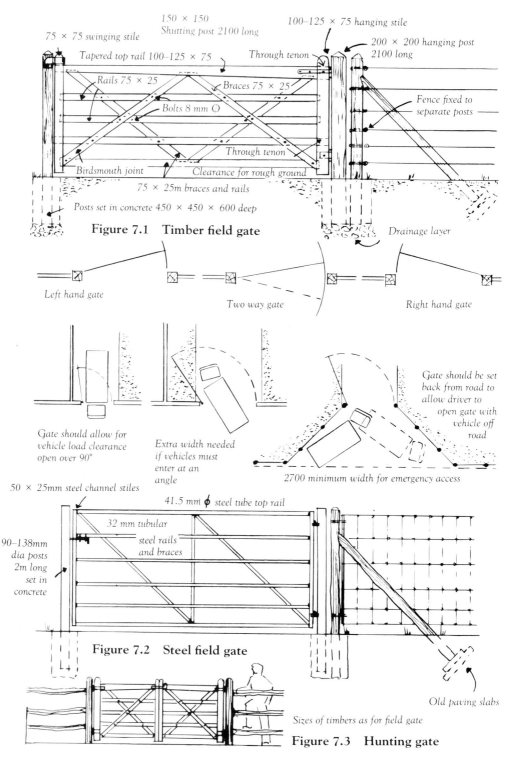

75 × 75 swinging stile

150 × 150
Shutting post 2100 long

100–125 × 75 hanging stile

200 × 200 hanging post
2100 long

Tapered top rail 100–125 × 75

Through tenon

Rails 75 × 25

Braces 75 × 25

Fence fixed to
separate posts

Bolts 8 mm ⌀

Through tenon

Birdsmouth joint

Clearance for rough ground

75 × 25m braces and rails

Posts set in concrete 450 × 450 × 600 deep

Drainage layer

Figure 7.1   Timber field gate

Left hand gate

Two way gate

Right hand gate

Gate should allow for
vehicle load clearance
open over 90°

Extra width needed
if vehicles must
enter at an
angle

Gate should be set
back from road to
allow driver to
open gate with
vehicle off
road

2700 minimum width for emergency access

50 × 25mm steel channel stiles

41.5 mm ⌀ steel tube top rail

32 mm tubular
steel rails
and braces

90–138mm
dia posts
2m long
set in
concrete

Figure 7.2   Steel field gate

Old paving slabs

Sizes of timbers as for field gate

Figure 7.3   Hunting gate

152

usually has less ornamental furniture. Tubular steel gates are very basic, but sturdy and comparatively cheap, as although they cannot be repaired on site the cost of replacement is low. Timber gates may be treated with preservative only, painted or stained, while steel gates are galvanized and may also be painted. BS 4092: parts 1 and 2:1966 describe the requirements for small domestic gates of metal and timber, but as these do not usually form part of a landscape contract they are not discussed here and the principles of construction are similar to those of field and entrance gates.

Timber field gates

Field gates are, as their name implies, intended to close openings into agricultural fields, but they may be used for car parks, parks storage depots, and similar areas where a rural appearance is required. They are specified in BS 3470:1975. When in doubt about the correct width of gate, choose one larger than seems to be necessary, and if wider gates than 4200 mm are needed, a pair of gates must be used since increasing the size of the timbers will only strain the hinges and hanging post. Where access for fire services is a requirement the minimum width is 2700 mm. Typical field gate sizes are 2400, 2700, 3000, 3300, 3600, 3900, and 4200 mm wide, and 1100 mm or 1300 mm high. Most field gates are 'diamond braced' which allows them to be hung from either side, though better quality gates have a larger hanging stile for strength and the top rail is tapered to reduce the weight. The timbers for a standard treated softwood field gate would be top rail 125 × 75 mm tapered from hanging to swinging side, other rails and braces 75 × 25 mm, swinging stile 75 × 75 mm and hanging stile 125 × 75 mm. Both the rails and the braces should be morticed into the stiles and the crossing points of the rails and braces should be bolted with rust-resistant bolts. Field gates are usually hung to open both ways as neither horses nor tractors are very good at backing away from an opening gate, and they should be capable of opening more than 90° if possible to avoid damage from vehicles. The landscape designer should set out the gate-swings carefully, making allowance for any sight lines required by the highway authority, and if the approach to the gate is at an angle, allowance should be made for vehicles and trailers having to turn as they enter. Whether manual or electronically controlled, all entrance gates should be set well back from the public highway so that vehicles do not have to stop on the road while the gate is being opened; the actual distance for the set-back will depend on the maximum overall length of vehicles using the site (See Figure 7.1.).

Steel field gates

These are also covered in BS 3470:1975. For utilitarian work the tubular steel field gate is a durable alternative to the timber gate as it is less liable to damage and requires no maintenance, and because of its comparatively light construction it can be used for wider openings than the timber gate. Typical sizes are

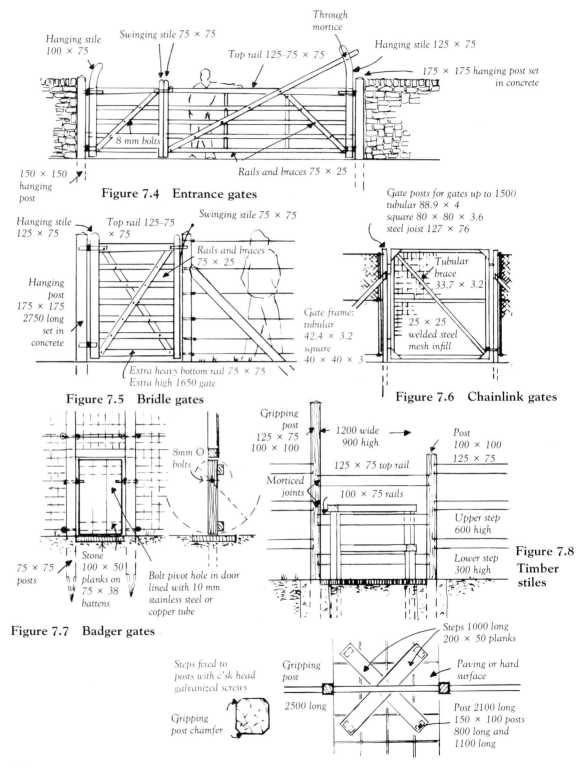

Figure 7.4 Entrance gates

Hanging stile 100 × 75
Swinging stile 75 × 75
Through mortice
Top rail 125–75 × 75
Hanging stile 125 × 75
175 × 175 hanging post set in concrete
8 mm bolts
Rails and braces 75 × 25
150 × 150 hanging post

Figure 7.5 Bridle gates

Hanging stile 125 × 75
Top rail 125–75 × 75
Swinging stile 75 × 75
Rails and braces 75 × 25
Hanging post 175 × 175 2750 long set in concrete
Extra heavy bottom rail 75 × 75
Extra high 1650 gate

Figure 7.6 Chainlink gates

Gate posts for gates up to 1500
tubular 88.9 × 4
square 80 × 80 × 3.6
steel joist 127 × 76
Tubular brace 33.7 × 3.2
Gate frame: tubular 42.4 × 3.2
square 40 × 40 × 3
25 × 25 welded steel mesh infill

Figure 7.7 Badger gates

8mm O bolts
Stone 100 × 50 planks on 75 × 38 battens
75 × 75 posts
Bolt pivot hole in door lined with 10 mm stainless steel or copper tube

Figure 7.8 Timber stiles

Gripping post 125 × 75 100 × 100
1200 wide 900 high
Post 100 × 100 125 × 75
125 × 75 top rail
Morticed joints
100 × 75 rails
Upper step 600 high
Lower step 300 high

Steps fixed to posts with c'sk head galvanized screws
Gripping post chamfer
Gripping post 2500 long
Steps 1000 long 200 × 50 planks
Paving or hard surface
Post 2100 long 150 × 100 posts 800 long and 1100 long

154

2400, 3000, 3300, 3600, 4200, and 4600 mm wide and 1150 mm high. Heavy duty or cattle-yard gates are manufactured with six rails of 41.5 mm and 32 mm welded tubular steel galvanized, with 50 × 25 mm steel channel stiles and 2 m long steel posts from 90 to 138 mm diameter, and come complete with furniture. Lighter field gates for general farm use are made from 26.9 mm tubular steel and have lighter posts of 60 mm to 89mm diameter. The hanging post is always larger than the shutting post (See Figure 7.2).

Hunting gates

'Hunting gates' are similar in construction to field gates, but they are supplied in two leaves so that a horseman does not have to back his mount the full length of a field gate when opening it. Widths are 900, 1200, 1500, 1800, 2100 mm each (See Figure 7.3).

Entrance Gates

Drive or entrance gates are usually made of hardwood for the sake of appearance and are left natural colour. Sizes of gates and timbers are similar to those of field gates, but all timbers are planed smooth with the top rail and the stiles being chamfered. A more ornate type of entrance gate has a tall curved hanging stile with one long and one short diagonal brace (See Figure 7.4).

Bridle or horse gates

Horse gates are similar in sizes and construction to field gates, but manufactured in hardwood, and they open one way only. They are seven rails high in order to prevent active horses from jumping them and to allow riders to reach the latches easily, and they have a rather heavier construction with hanging and shutting stiles of 125 × 75 mm and 75 × 75 mm respectively, top rail 125 × 75 mm, and bottom rail 75 × 75 mm with gate posts 175 × 175 mm and 125 × 125 mm for hanging and shutting posts respectively, set 750 mm in the ground. All joints should be morticed and tenoned. BS 5709:1979 specifies a width of 1525 mm and a height of 1100 mm which is on the low side for anything larger than a twelve-hand pony, but typical commercial sizes are single 1200, double 3000 and 3600 mm wide × 1650 mm high (See Figure 7.5).

Chain-link gates

Gates for chain-link fencing are made to match the fence in height and mesh type. The construction is usually of mild steel angle similar to the steel angle posts described earlier, braced and welded at the corners and factory fitted with hinges and pad-bolts which are designed to take a padlock. Standard gate openings are 970 mm for a single leaf, but virtually any size may be manufactured to order in single or double leaf. As in the case of field gates, chain-link gates should be specified as opening 90° or 180° and the direction of opening

155

Plate 24 Entrance gate *This is an elegant version of the ordinary field gate. It is often made of hardwood, left natural or stained, and may incorporate a wicket gate for pedestrians. The massive hardwood gateposts are independent of the adjoining wall. Entrance gates are usually made to swing in both directions.*

should always be given. Chain-link gates are very liable to abuse from climbing or kicking, and it is advisable to use a heavy welded-mesh infill in preference to ordinary chain-link. Welded mesh is manufactured in a range of sizes from 900 mm high × 50 × 50 mm mesh made of 2.5 mm thick wire, to 3 m high × 75 × 25 mm mesh made of 3.0 mm thick wire. Square and rectangular patterns are available (See Figure 7.6).

7.2 BADGER GATES

Where badgers are prolific, and their immutable ancestral routes run through a boundary fence, it will be necessary to provide badger gates if the fence is not to be removed by these strong and obstinate animals. An active badger can uproot 2 m concrete posts in concrete footings and can climb a 2 m brick wall without difficulty. The gate should be 300 mm wide and 500 mm high, pivoting on 8 mm bolts at two-thirds of its height from the ground so that it closes automatically. The gate should be made of 100 × 50 mm planks battened together and the top bar and gate posts should be 75 × 75 mm timbers driven well into the ground. The gate should be heavy enough to prevent rabbits and game birds from using it, and the ground under the gate should be concreted or paved to prevent digging. Although small dogs are able to get through the gate they tend not to do so because of the force required to push them open (See Figure 7.7).

7.3   STILES AND KISSING GATES

Though not strictly gates, stiles and kissing gates are a useful alternative to pedestrian gates where stock control is important. Stiles may be timber or prefabricated galvanized tubular steel, and they should be provided with extra posts designed to take way-marks or notices which should be vandal proof; the traditional round signposts with clip-on direction signs should be avoided since they give much entertainment to local lads who swivel the signs round and make navigating extremely difficult for the wayfarer.

Timber stiles

BS 5709:1979 gives recommended sizes and construction of timber stiles. A better quality stile would be constructed of two posts 100 × 100 mm or 125 × 75 mm, one 2 m long and one 3 m long with the arrises chamfered or rounded to provide a hand-grip and set 750 mm into the ground. The 125 × 75 mm top rail should be no higher than 900 mm and the other two 100 × 75 mm rails should be spaced equally. The two steps, set at right angles to each other, are made of 200 × 50 mm planks supported by 150 × 100 mm posts; they must not rest on the rails as this is bad for both the step and the rail. The stile may be treated softwood or hardwood, though the timbers should not be treated with any preservative which is likely to damage clothing, and all arrises should be rounded to prevent splintering. The stile should be at least 1200 mm wide and the steps not less than 1000 mm long to allow plenty of room for walkers with large packs and those with physical difficulties. The maximum rise should be 300mm, which may involve making up the adjacent ground and the top rail should not be more than 600 mm above the top step. All rails should be morticed into the posts, and bolts and coach screws should be used to connect the members. Unless the ground is very firm all posts should be set in concrete footings and the ground under and adjacent to the stile should be paved or gravelled to prevent slipping. These stiles can be made from local small timber and can easily be made up by volunteer labour as part of a conservation project. If signs or notices are required they should be fixed to separate posts so that they cannot hit a walker's head (See Figure 7.8).

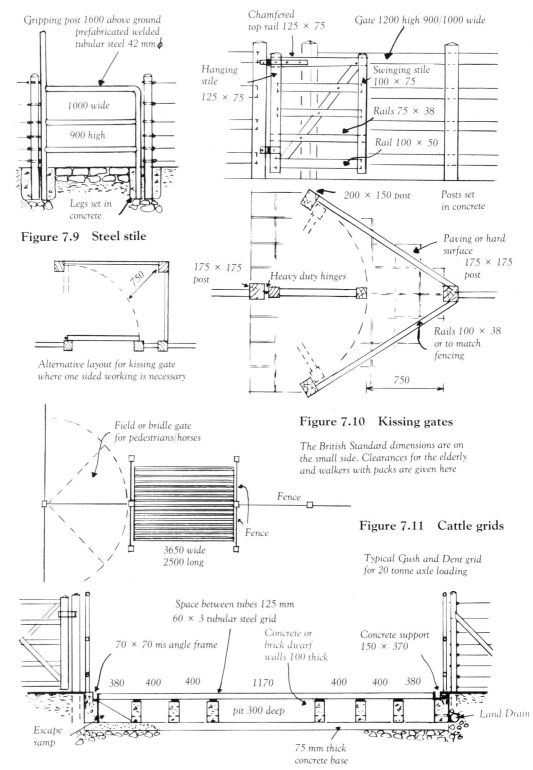

Gripping post 1600 above ground
prefabricated welded
tubular steel 42 mm φ

1000 wide

900 high

Legs set in
concrete

Figure 7.9   Steel stile

Chamfered
top rail 125 × 75

Gate 1200 high 900/1000 wide

Hanging
stile
125 × 75

Swinging stile
100 × 75

Rails 75 × 38

Rail 100 × 50

Posts set
in concrete

200 × 150 post

Paving or hard
surface
175 × 175
post

175 × 175
post

Heavy duty hinges

Rails 100 × 38
or to match
fencing

750

Alternative layout for kissing gate
where one sided working is necessary

750

Figure 7.10   Kissing gates

The British Standard dimensions are on
the small side. Clearances for the elderly
and walkers with packs are given here

Field or bridle gate
for pedestrians/horses

Fence

Fence

3650 wide
2500 long

Figure 7.11   Cattle grids

Typical Gush and Dent grid
for 20 tonne axle loading

Space between tubes 125 mm
60 × 3 tubular steel grid

70 × 70 ms angle frame

Concrete or
brick dwarf
walls 100 thick

Concrete support
150 × 370

380   400   400   1170   400   400   380

pit 300 deep

Escape
ramp

Land Drain

75 mm thick
concrete base

158

Tubular steel stiles

Prefabricated tubular steel stiles are similar in design and height to the timber stiles, but are manufactured in one piece with rails to step on rather than with projecting steps, and they are less negotiable than step stiles for the elderly walker (See Figure 7.9).

Kissing gates

Kissing gates are briefly described in BS 5709:1979 but the dimensions given are on the small side. The kissing gate is a very traditional gate for pedestrians who cannot climb stiles and where stock control is important; they are also a useful barrier to bicycles (though these can be lifted over the gate) and motorbicycles. They do, however, prevent access by prams, landscape machinery, and wheelchairs unless combined with a field gate which may be opened for special users, so that the client must be required to confirm (in writing) that this is his intention before kissing gates are specified.

As for ordinary gates, kissing gates may be prefabricated of steel tube and bar, obtained as prefabricated units for assembly on site, or made on site from stock timber. The gate itself is a standard small five-barred field gate 900 mm or 1000 mm wide by 1200 mm high with chamfered or rounded arrises, hung on centre-pin hinges to swing both ways, and the hinges should be substantial since kissing gates offer an attractive swing to children. The four posts of treated softwood or hardwood are 200 × 150 mm and 175 × 175 mm, 2200 mm long and with one extra post at the end of the enclosure 3500 mm long to carry signs, which are all set in concrete footings, since the gate is often slammed back and forth with considerable force. Although the BS recommends a clear area of 500 mm^2 to pass the end of the gate it is better that the enclosure should provide at least 750 mm clearance to allow for pedestrians with large packs and parents with small children. The gate is constructed of five rails morticed into the posts which need to be substantial to withstand children climbing on them. As for stiles, the area inside and adjacent to the kissing gate should be paved or gravelled, and all top rails and end posts should have their arrises rounded to prevent splintering. A kissing gate does not normally have any latch or bolt, but a galvanized steel strap hasp and staple may be fitted to enable the gate to be padlocked (See Figure 7.10 and Plate 25).

7.4   CATTLE GRIDS

Cattle grids on private roads which will carry vehicles up to 10.16 tonnes are described in BS 4008:1973. These stock barriers are used in the South of England to control access to open land such as the New Forest, Dartmoor and Exmoor and more generally in the North of England and Scotland for farm gateways. Although very intelligent and hungry horses and ponies can cross it

Plate 25   Cattle grid and kissing gate   *A small cattle grid designed for access to a field adjoining a public open space where people cannot be relied on to shut gates. A cattle grid also allows drivers of farm vehicles to turn off and onto the road without stopping to open gates. The kissing gate is a barrier to animals, and on its own it is a barrier to motorbikes, but it is passable by pedestrians. The height bar over the grid prevents caravans from entering the field.*

by rolling over, it provides a good barrier to sheep, cattle and deer while allowing vehicles and pedestrians to travel through without the delay of open- ing and shutting gates, and is very suitable for country parks and common-land gateways. The grid is made of prefabricated tubular steel bar units or flat- topped bars, or channel sections with gaps, assembled on site. The grid should be specified to carry the expected weight of vehicle. A typical small cattle grid would be 2750 mm wide and 2600 mm long which will deter farm stock, though where red deer are to be controlled the grid should be 3500 mm long. Grids are not made for two vehicles to pass on the grid. For public roads the highway engineer should be consulted as to the correct foundations and wall construction for the pit; for lightly trafficked private roads the concrete retain- ing walls should be 100 mm thick on concrete foundations and may have to be reinforced if heavy traffic is expected. The pit should be not less than 300 mm deep to allow for debris to clear the bars, and drainage from the pit must be provided, together with a narrow sloping concrete ramp leading out of the pit to enable small mammals such as hedgehogs to escape. The pit should be regularly cleared and treated with herbicide. Intermediate concrete supports are provided at spacings which provide the maximum support under the wheels of vehicles. The dimensions between bar centres measured from the sides of the grid are:

- for grids of tubular steel or flat topped steel bars: 380 – 400 variable – 400 – 380 mm
- for grids of steel channels: 410 – 965 – variable – 965 – 410 mm. These supports should have a narrow top of 40 mm maximum so that sheep cannot walk along them.

The sides of the pit must be flush with the guard rails so that stock cannot creep along the edge of the pit. At the side of the cattle grid a field gate for riders and horse-and-cart traffic must be provided, and this should be self-closing. Cattle grids crossing a public road must be properly signposted to the requirements of the highway engineer and it is good practice to do the same for private roads and driveways (See Figure 7.11).

7.5   POLE BARRIERS

Pole barriers and removable posts are not strictly gates, though they perform many of the same functions, and they require very little in the way of construction to install them. They are supplied by specialist contractors in widths from 3 m to 8 m, and may be either simple counter-weighted poles raised and lowered by hand or more complex automatically controlled barriers with warning lights. The operation can be controlled by remote control from protected cabins, by inserting cards or coins in a control post, or by remote control from the approaching vehicle. Pole barriers must automatically fold upwards and fall upwards in the 'fail-safe' position so that vehicles or pedestrians are not injured in case of the mechanism failing. They should always be well lighted and for security applications they should be crash-proof. In public areas it may be desirable to specify the type that has a flexible wire mesh which fills the gap under the pole when it is closed; this prevents pedestrians from ducking under the closed barrier. The landscape designer should specify that the posts supporting the pole and its rest are to be set in concrete and he should also allow for an electric supply to the barrier for lighting and control mechanism if satisfactory public lighting does not already exist (See Figure 7.12).

7.6   GATE FURNITURE

The selection of the correct gate furniture is almost as important as the choice of gate itself as the wrong fittings may fail to make the gate function as it

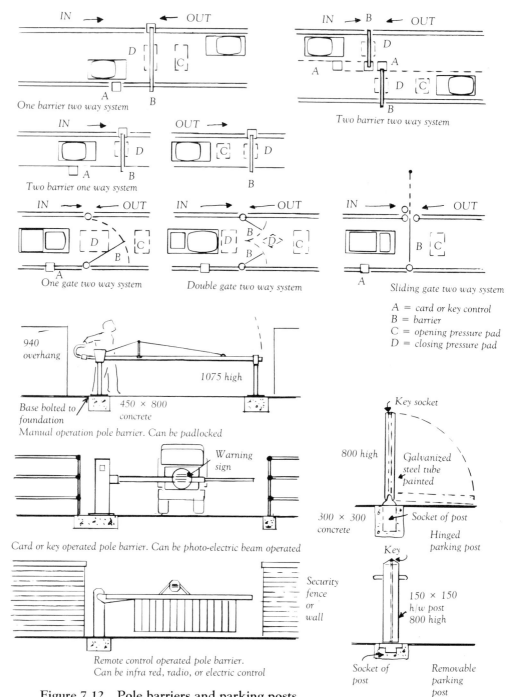

One barrier two way system

Two barrier two way system

IN → OUT →

Two barrier one way system

One gate two way system

Double gate two way system

Sliding gate two way system

A = card or key control
B = barrier
C = opening pressure pad
D = closing pressure pad

940 overhang

1075 high

Base bolted to foundation
450 × 800 concrete

Manual operation pole barrier. Can be padlocked

Warning sign

Card or key operated pole barrier. Can be photo-electric beam operated

Security fence or wall

Remote control operated pole barrier.
Can be infra red, radio, or electric control

Key socket

800 high

Galvanized steel tube painted

300 × 300 concrete

Socket of post

Hinged parking post

Key

150 × 150 h/w post
800 high

Socket of post

Removable parking post

Figure 7.12   Pole barriers and parking posts

Typical Barretts of Wroughton barriers

162

should, they may cease to work under heavy use, or they do not complement the design of the gate properly. Furniture may be considered under the headings of hinges, latches, and bolts and a gate may be fitted with two or more types according to its function. Light furniture is fixed with plated screws, and heavier furniture is fitted either with coach bolts which have a square section below a cup head which prevents them from turning in the wood, or coach screws which have a heavy square head turned with a spanner. Washers should be used under nuts to prevent them from being pulled into the wood. Set screws, which are bolts threaded the full length of the shaft, should not be used. Traditional gate furniture is made of wrought iron, and the genuine forged wrought iron is very tough and durable although rather expensive for cost-conscious clients; it should not be confused with the bent steel strip which passes for wrought iron in garden centres. It should be primed before fixing and painted after fixing. For ordinary landscape work and where cost is important, galvanized steel fittings are used; they should be hot-dipped after manufacture and not electro-galvanized as this process does not give a thick-enough coat of zinc. Stainless steel is an excellent material for fittings, and although there are very few gate and fence fittings available at present in stainless steel (except screws and bolts), these may become more popular in future.

Gate Hinges

Hinges are designed to carry loads ranging from the light palisade garden gate to the heaviest hardwood entrance gate or steel rail security gate. The most common types are as follows:

- *Tee hinge*; used for light garden gates opening one way only. They are made of pressed steel with the short plate fitted to the hanging post and the long tail fitted to the gate. Lengths of tail are 200, 300, 400, 450, and 600 mm. Galvanized or primed for painting. Rust-resistant screws should be used and the screw holes pre-drilled in hardwood gates.
- *Hook-and-band hinges*; used for medium weight gates. Galvanized strip steel , bolted to the gate and coach-screwed to the post. The hinges may be mounted both pins up where it is desirable to be able to lift the gate off its hinges, or one pin up and one down for gates which are not to be removed.
- *Reversible hinges*, which may be used for both left- and right-handed gates are heavier, and as the hinge pin is held to the post at both top and bottom, they are less likely to wear than the hook-and-band type. Light reversible hinges are 350 and 450 mm long; heavy ones are 600, 750, and 900 mm long for heavy entrance gates.
- *Double-band centre-pin hinges* are intended for gates which open in both directions. The hinge band is U-shaped to fit both sides of the top rail, and the bottom hinge may be either a single pin, or a double pin which

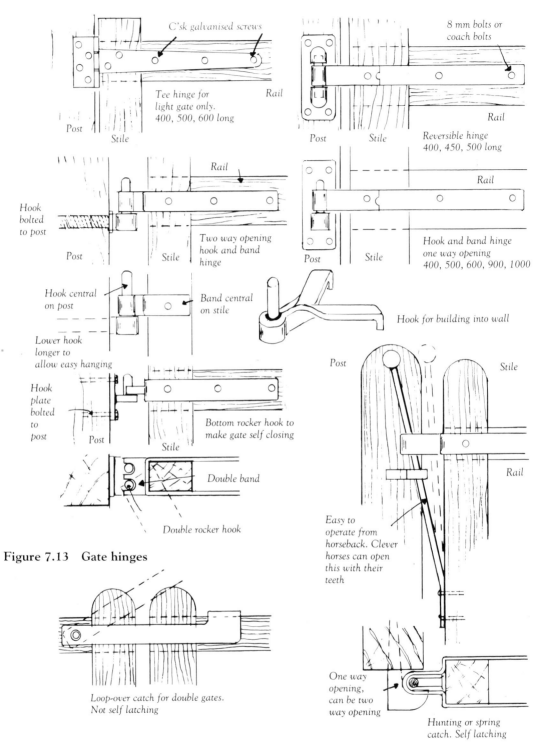

C'sk galvanised screws

Tee hinge for
light gate only.
400, 500, 600 long

Post

Stile

Rail

8 mm bolts or
coach bolts

Post   Stile

Rail

Reversible hinge
400, 450, 500 long

Hook
bolted
to post

Rail

Two way opening
hook and band
hinge

Post

Stile

Rail

Post   Stile

Hook and band hinge
one way opening
400, 500, 600, 900, 1000

Hook central
on post

Band central
on stile

Hook for building into wall

Lower hook
longer to
allow easy hanging

Hook
plate
bolted
to
post

Post

Stile

Bottom rocker hook to
make gate self closing

Post

Stile

Rail

Double band

Double rocker hook

Easy to
operate from
horseback. Clever
horses can open
this with their
teeth

One way
opening,
can be two
way opening

Hunting or spring
catch. Self latching

Figure 7.13   Gate hinges

Loop-over catch for double gates.
Not self latching

Figure 7.14(a)   Gate latches and catches

164

acts as a self-closer to bring the gate back to the centre position (See Figure 7.13).

Gate latches and catches

Latches or catches for gates were traditionally designed to keep the gate fastened against persistent and intelligent horses and cattle, but to be easily opened by horsemen or cold and stiff farmworkers, so they are made with large hand grips and are hung so as to be either self-closing or easy to shut from either side (See Figure 7.14). The most common types are as follows:

- *One-way auto catch*; a U-bolt closing into a weighted catch which is opened by lifting the catch. There is no adjustment for gate movement, so this catch is not suitable for heavily used gates. Light versions of this catch are used on garden gates with a projecting arm engaging with a weighted catch.
- *Self-weighted latch*; suitable for two-way gates; the operating arm is within the thickness of the gate and not easily accessible for riders.
- *Hunting latch*; a long arm projecting above the gate is easily reached from horseback. The arm is springy enough to return itself into the catch after opening.
- A *loop-over latch* is intended to fasten a pair of gates, and is simply a loop of metal pivoting on one gate and dropping over the other. It is not self-closing, and is therefore not suitable for public footpaths.
- In order to keep the gate open while traffic passes through, *counter weighted gate catches* should be fitted at the rear of the gate swing; they catch the gate automatically when it is opened and are released by pushing down the counter-weight with the foot.

Most types of gates can be fitted with automatic opening and closing devices controlled by photo-electric cells or push-buttons set clear of the gate swing, or by remote control by the driver. Electronic locking can be added to this equipment which is supplied either by mains or battery electricity. Remember that such gate controls may have to be operated by the emergency services, so the landscape designer should check with these services before specifying electronic controls. The gates should also be capable of being opened and shut if the controls go wrong. (See Figures 7.14a and 7.14b).

Gate bolts

Bolts are used to hold one of a pair of gates while the other is in use, or to hold gates open instead of gate catches. Because gates are heavily and often roughly used, bolt shoes or sockets should allow plenty of room for movement. The best type of socket is the boat or half-round socket which allows debris to be swept out of it; a small round hole is useless as a bolt socket. Gate bolts are long in order to keep the handles out of the mud, and are either

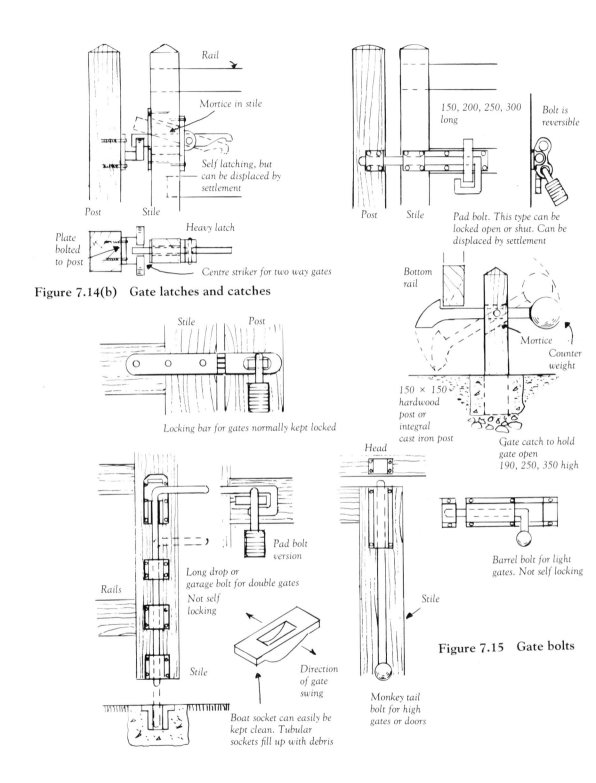

Rail

Mortice in stile

Self latching, but can be displaced by settlement

Post   Stile

Plate bolted to post

Heavy latch

Centre striker for two way gates

Figure 7.14(b)   Gate latches and catches

150, 200, 250, 300 long

Bolt is reversible

Post   Stile

Pad bolt. This type can be locked open or shut. Can be displaced by settlement

Stile   Post

Locking bar for gates normally kept locked

Bottom rail

Mortice

Counter weight

150 × 150 hardwood post or integral cast iron post

Gate catch to hold gate open 190, 250, 350 high

Head

Pad bolt version

Long drop or garage bolt for double gates

Not self locking

Rails

Stile

Barrel bolt for light gates. Not self locking

Direction of gate swing

Stile

Boat socket can easily be kept clean. Tubular sockets fill up with debris

Monkey tail bolt for high gates or doors

Figure 7.15   Gate bolts

monkey-tailed with a knob on top, or drop-bolts with a right angled handle which may be padlocked. Gates are locked by means of a pad-bolt which has a perforated flange on the bolt and a fixed staple which carries the padlock, as ordinary mortice or rim locks are not weatherproof and do not have enough tolerance in the latch movement. It is important to check that the pad-bolt fixing bolts cannot be undone easily when the gate is locked. Locking bars based on the hasp-and-staple principle may also be used. These fastenings can be simple galvanized steel strip, or tool-proof hardened steel with secret fixings for security gates, and the landscape designer should check the client's requirements before specifying locking devices. (See Figure 7.15).

8   RAILINGS

Railings may be considered as a superior type of fence since they perform much the same function but in a more elegant way. There are also special barriers designed to prevent pedestrians and vehicles from coming into contact with each other, but these are usually specified by a highway engineer and would only enter a landscape contract as part of a car- or lorry-parking project.

8.1   RAILING TYPES

There are two main types of railings; the horizontal rail and stanchion type and the vertical bar railing type which are mostly made to order, based on a selection of standard designs fabricated into panels for each contract to the exact size and shape required. Firms such as Dorothea specialize in highly ornamental cast-iron railings and features for restoration or replica work, but these attractive items are very expensive and the majority of landscape designers will have to be content with plain cast-iron or steel railings. The line between railings and security fencing is not easily drawn, since most high railings offer some degree of security and conversely some security fencing is so well designed as to perform the function of ornamental railings; the landscape designer should be quite clear which function takes priority in his design.

Traditionally, railings are constructed with each baluster set individually into the stone or concrete base, as this makes for the strongest construction, but even when the balusters are run in lead into the socket the corrosive effect of rainwater running down the metal will eventually destroy the metal at its base. To prevent this happening it is better to weld the balusters to a bottom rail which is fixed into the side of the supporting posts or piers, though this construction does mean that the supports will have to be closer together than they need be if the balusters were individually fixed.

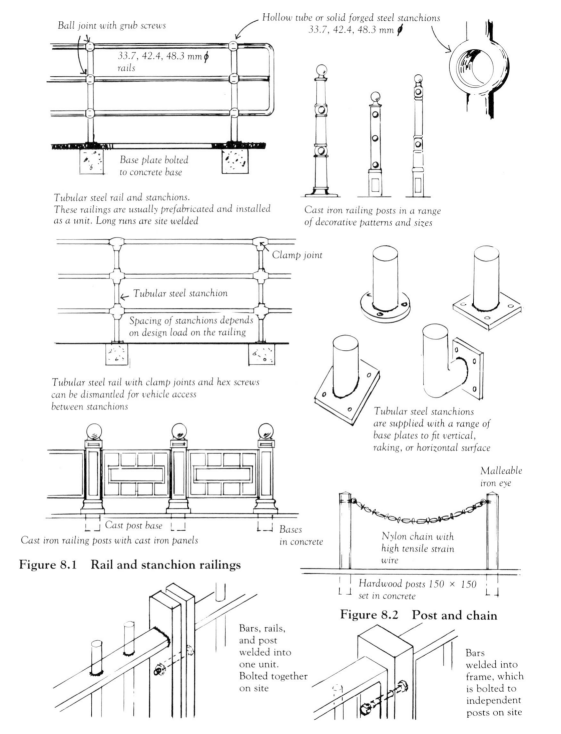

Ball joint with grub screws

Hollow tube or solid forged steel stanchions
33.7, 42.4, 48.3 mm ⌀

33.7, 42.4, 48.3 mm ⌀
rails

Base plate bolted
to concrete base

Tubular steel rail and stanchions.
These railings are usually prefabricated and installed
as a unit. Long runs are site welded

Cast iron railing posts in a range
of decorative patterns and sizes

Clamp joint

Tubular steel stanchion

Spacing of stanchions depends
on design load on the railing

Tubular steel rail with clamp joints and hex screws
can be dismantled for vehicle access
between stanchions

Tubular steel stanchions
are supplied with a range of
base plates to fit vertical,
raking, or horizontal surface

Cast post base

Bases
in concrete

Cast iron railing posts with cast iron panels

Figure 8.1   Rail and stanchion railings

Malleable
iron eye

Nylon chain with
high tensile strain
wire

Hardwood posts 150 × 150
set in concrete

Figure 8.2   Post and chain

Bars, rails,
and post
welded into
one unit.
Bolted together
on site

Bars
welded into
frame, which
is bolted to
independent
posts on site

Figure 8.3(a)   Vertical bar railings

170

Rail and stanchion railings

Rail and stanchion railings are associated with seaside promenades, ships, and canals in the public mind and they are a suitable choice for any waterside design – though where there is a danger of falling over or through them a more substantial barrier is required, which may consist of prefabricated panels of heavy welded wire mesh fixed between the rails. They consist of square or round rail posts with tubular rails passed through holes in the posts. The posts themselves are more or less ornamental, ranging from plain vertical shafts with ball connections to highly decorated posts with fluted shafts and moulded caps, bases and connections which may be picked out in colour. Heights of posts range from 650 mm with one trip rail to 1240 mm high posts with three or four rails, and the diameters of the posts range from 33.7 mm to 120 mm; the larger sizes should be specified where there is a risk of damage by waves or vehicles. Since railings are most often used in paved areas, the posts are set in concrete footings at 1 m to 2 m centres, and some types have a bolt-down flange set horizontally or at an angle as well as or instead of a sunk base. Cast iron is the traditional material for ornamental rail posts but they can be made in cast aluminium if weight is a consideration, while the utilitarian types are made of tubular steel 33.7, 42.4, and 48.3 mm outside diameter and of forged steel 32 and 38 mm o/d. Newer materials now coming on the market offer the strength of cast iron with the malleability of wrought iron, but the range of designs of these is limited at present. The rails are made of heavy gauge tubular steel to BS 6323 and 1387 in the same sizes as the rail posts, and are fixed to the posts by recessed screws. These railings may be galvanized, primed for site painting or powder colour-coated, and prefabricated bends and angles are manufactured (See Figure 8.1).

Post and chain railings

Rail posts carrying chains are a version of this type but do not provide much of a barrier since they can be lifted or jumped over, and if they are to be used the chain must be fixed to posts with hammer-over eyes. The strongest chain is heavy galvanized steel, but this is unsuitable in vandal prone areas as the chain can be removed and used as a really destructive weapon. It is preferable to use heavy-gauge nylon chain with high-tensile multiple-strand stainless steel wire threaded through each link, as unreinforced nylon chain has a site life measured in hours or even less when installed close to schools. Chain railings are best suited to restoration work or to protected sites where a classical effect is wanted. When chain railings are used as car parking barriers, a clear space of 1m should be left for pedestrian access at the rear of the chain. (See Figure 8.2).

Vertical bar railings

Vertical bar railings consist of mild-steel or cast-iron balusters in plain or ornamental patterns, passing through horizontal rails, and finished with plain

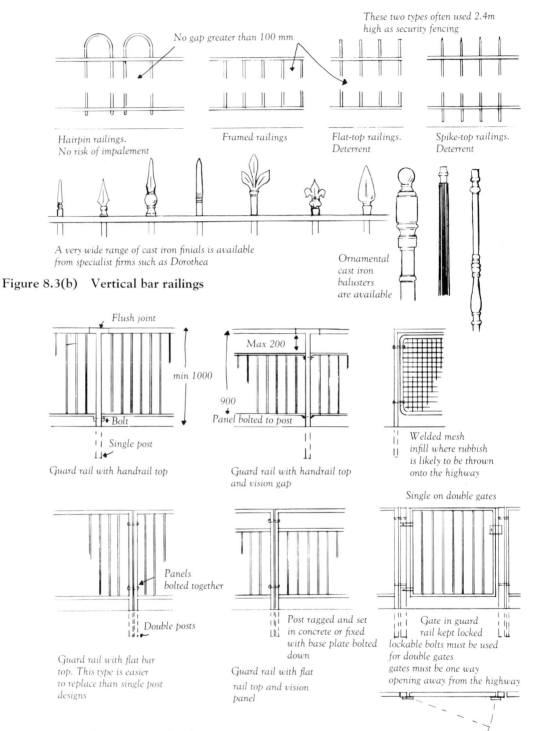

These two types often used 2.4m high as security fencing

No gap greater than 100 mm

Hairpin railings.
No risk of impalement

Framed railings

Flat-top railings.
Deterrent

Spike-top railings.
Deterrent

A very wide range of cast iron finials is available
from specialist firms such as Dorothea

Ornamental
cast iron
balusters
are available

Figure 8.3(b)   Vertical bar railings

Flush joint

min 1000

Bolt

Single post

Guard rail with handrail top

Max 200

900

Panel bolted to post

Guard rail with handrail top
and vision gap

Welded mesh
infill where rubbish
is likely to be thrown
onto the highway

Single on double gates

Panels
bolted together

Double posts

Guard rail with flat bar
top. This type is easier
to replace than single post
designs

Post ragged and set
in concrete or fixed
with base plate bolted
down

Guard rail with flat
rail top and vision
panel

Gate in guard
rail kept locked
lockable bolts must be used
for double gates
gates must be one way
opening away from the highway

Figure 8.4   Pedestrian guard railings

172

Plate 26   Vertical bar railings   *Panels of pre-fabricated hairpin railings concreted into the ground and bolted together with an intermediate supporting stub post. These railings cannot impale people, and are useful for playgrounds or other areas where children or adults are likely to push each other about.*

or ornamental finials; they are usually prefabricated in panels for site erection. Supporting posts at 2 m centres may be plain or highly ornamented and are provided with ragged bases for concreting in or flanged bases for bolting down. Finials may be blunt-topped or bow-topped where there is a danger of impalement, otherwise the cast iron spear, lance, fleur-de-lys, trefoil or other pattern may be used. In addition to single balusters, panels of ornamental cast-iron work may be used between posts. Balusters must be not more than 100 mm apart in order to prevent children from getting their heads trapped. These railings are usually supplied primed for site painting. BS 1722:Pt 9:1979 specifies a range of standard vertical bar railings. All posts should be at 2760 mm centres (See Table 8.1 and Figure 8.3(a) and (b).).

Plate 27 Vertical bar railings   *Plain vertical bars welded to top and bottom rails which are then welded to posts set in a stone coping. The gates are made to match. These railings are not a security fence, but simply form an identifiable enclosure which prevents vehicles and casual pedestrians from entering.*

Table 8.1
British Standard vertical bar railings

Situation	Size of bars round or square	Size of posts and horizontal rails	Height
Gardens	16 mm	35 × 10 mm	1200 mm
Housing fences, gardens	16 mm	35 × 10 mm	1350 mm
Housing fences, gardens	19 mm	40 × 10 mm	1500 mm
Parks, public gardens	19 mm	40 × 10 mm	1650 mm
Schools, parks, horse paddocks	19 mm	40 × 10 mm	1800 mm
Light security	22 mm	50 × 10 mm	1950 mm
Security fence	22 mm	50 × 10 mm	2100 mm

Plate 28   Vertical bar railings   *Formal mild steel railings with ornamental cast iron heads. The vertical bars are passed through the flat horizontal rails and the decorative bracing and welded. The rails are more elegant to build the horizontal rails directly into the brickwork, but the angle fixing allows a damaged railing section to be replaced. Formal railings are usually painted black with the heads gilded, though bright strong red, blue or dark green can be used effectively.*

8.2   PROTECTIVE BARRIERS

This section does not cover the design and installation of highway barriers intended to control fast-moving heavy vehicles, as this is the province of the highway engineer. Where the landscape designer is concerned with the interchange of vehicles and pedestrians in the immediate vicinity of buildings, it will be necessary to provide protective barriers to pedestrian areas and access points in projects involving public access such as shopping centres, schools, sports centres, and superstores; these are typical projects where pedestrian protection is required. BS 6180:1982 gives recommendations for the design of barriers to resist vehicular impacts of different intensities. Such barriers should be designed without projections which would prevent a vehicle from being deflected along them on impact. Ideally, it should be difficult to climb over, fall through, or get trapped in barriers, and they should obviously have no sharp edges or spikes likely to cause damage to people or clothing.

Where vehicles are entering or leaving access points protected by barriers, reflective signs and very clear warning signs should be provided, both for the pedestrians and the drivers; though on public roads the highway authorities are responsible for providing signs, on private roads the building owner is responsible. The whole system of pedestrian and vehicle routes, barriers, and signposting should be considered at the design stage in close consultation with the client and in particular the expected weights and speeds of vehicles entering the site must be determined.

When within the building curtilage, a barrier protecting pedestrians from access roads, sunken areas, or basements, must be:

- capable of withstanding a maximum combined wind and vehicle uniformly distributed load of 1.0 kN/m run at 1100 mm above its base;
- capable of withstanding a point load on the infill panel of 1.0 k/N;
- capable of withstanding a uniformly distributed load on the infill panel of 1.0 kN/m^2;
- not less than 1100 mm above its base; and,
- where children are at risk, openings in the barrier should be not greater than 100 mm in order to avoid trapping heads; and
- fixings and fastenings must be capable of withstanding the same loading as the barrier itself.

Pedestrian guard railings

Recommendations for pedestrian guard railings are given in BS 3049:1976, which classifies guard rails into the following three categories:

1 Class A for normal use; the rails must withstand 700N/m and the infill panels 500N/m.
2 Class B where vandalism is expected; the rails must withstand 700N/m and the panels 1000N/m.
3 Class C where crowd pressure is likely: rails must withstand 1400 N/m and panels 1000N/m.

Guard rails consist of plain round mild-steel bars welded top and bottom to flat rails, forming panels which are bolted to plain square or round tubular steel posts. Although the panels must not be easily removable, they may have to be removed for road works or replacement after traffic accidents, so they are not irremovably fixed. Instead of open steel bars, welded-mesh panels may be used where there is a danger of balls or rubbish falling through the bars, but, whatever the infill, drivers must be able to see people and objects

Plate 29 Pedestrian guard rails   *These are manufactured to British Standards controlling height, construction, and the sizes and spacings of bars; therefore the landscape designer has little choice in the design. Special designs may be permitted by the local authority if they comply with the Standard in all respects, but the landscape designer should check this before specifying non-standard guard rails.*

through the guard rails. A typical specification for a vehicle/pedestrian barrier would be posts at 2 m centres, distance from top to bottom rail 900 mm, ground clearance 150 mm maximum, height 1000 mm minimum, with four $75 \times 50 \times 3.15$ mm horizontal rolled hollow-steel rails 267 mm apart on $100 \times 100 \times 4.00$ mm posts, with welded-mesh infill panels secured to the rails (See Figure 8.4).

Gates in pedestrian barriers are manufactured to the same design as the barriers themselves and are usually the same width and height as the barrier panel. Single gates are required for light maintenance access to the protected area, and double gates where plant and vehicles must have access, and no gate may open onto the carriageway. All gates in a contract should have the same key or be master-keyed and in a local authority contract the locks may have to be to a standard pattern. Many barrier access gates may have to be opened in a hurry (and perhaps in darkness) by the emergency services, so they should be wide enough for fire engines and rescue vehicles. The fire brigade, the ambulance service, and the police should be consulted before gates and locks are specified in these situations.

9 PRESERVATIVE TREATMENT AND PAINTING

Both metal and timber may be treated with a single-process finish such as galvanizing or creosoting, or they may be finished with a paint system which usually consists of a primer whose function is to key into the surface and thus provide a sound base for subsequent coats, one or two undercoats whose function is to provide body colour and to obliterate any basic colour of the material, and one or two topcoats which provide a weather- and damage-proof surface and the final colour required by the landscape designer or his client.

9.1 TIMBER TREATMENT

Timber may be either left as treated in the works, or painted on site, or a combination of both. Local timber from an estate yard may be dipped in an open tank of preservative but this is not so satisfactory as pressure impregnation. Fencing and gate components are kiln-dried so that the natural sap is removed down to a specified moisture content, and then they are treated with preservative in special processes. Timber preservation may be classed as type A which should last for 40 years, and type B which should last for 20 years; for type A only the full-cell process and double vacuum processes are adequate and the immersion or pressure processes are not sufficient. For type B pressure and double-vacuum processes are satisfactory. No simple immersion technique can provide adequate protection, although tank-dipping is often used for estate work such as plantation fencing where long life is not essential. Where timber is to be in contact with water for prolonged periods it must be either a heavy hardwood such as jarrah, greenheart, or iroko, or it must be type A preservation treatment applied to redwood, pitch pine, larch, elm, beech and Douglas fir. BS 5589:1989 specifies the most suitable types of treatment for fencing and gate timber related to the location and the type of timber; broadly, timber in contact with the ground such as gate and fence posts should be type A and above-ground timbers such as gates and fence rails may be type B. The main preservatives are:

- creosote (tar oil) pressure process;
- creosote immersion process;
- creosote open-tank process;
- copper/chromium/arsenic (CCA) full-cell process;
- organic solvent (OC) double-vacuum process;
- organic solvent immersion process; and
- pentachlorophenol (PCP) in heavy oil double-vacuum process.

Creosote
Creosote to BS 144:1973 is suitable for open-tank or pressure treatment; it offers good resistance to damp but should be thoroughly dry before planting is carried out close to creosoted timber. Always light or dark brown, and cannot be painted over until the preservative is completely weathered.Low viscosity creosote to BS 3051 is intended for brush-applied work on site.

Organic solvent preservatives
The organic solvent preservatives, copper napthenate to BS 5056:1974 which is suitable for timber which is to be painted after treatment, and pentachloro-phenol (for timber not to be painted) to BS 5707: Pt 3: 1980 are much cleaner than creosote. These preservatives can be painted over as though they were unpainted but the solvent must be allowed to evaporate completely and only compatible paints can be used.

Water-borne preservatives
The water-borne preservatives such as copper/chromium/arsenic to BS 4072:Pt 2:1987 are resistant to leaching and can be painted after treatment but they are less used than the organic solvent preservatives. These types are almost colourless and can accept most paint colours, but they increase the moisture content of the timber and must be allowed to dry off properly before painting. It is wise to specify that the preservative is tinted so that the preservation can be checked by inspection on site, as 'invisible' preservative may be like the 'Emperor's new clothes'.

Timber finishes
Most proprietary solvent-based wood treatments contain fungicides and biocide, are made in various shades of light to dark brown, and the majority

of them are harmless to plants when completely dry. They may be transparent, opaque, or semi-opaque, and some are intended for finished surfaces while others are only suitable for rough-sawn timber. Timber to be stained should have a moisture content not higher than 20 per cent; timber to be painted should be equally dry and should be planed and sanded, free of grease, dust or any other contaminant and should not be painted in wet, very hot, or frosty weather. Softwoods may be primed with white or pink primer and hardwoods or resinous woods are primed with aluminium primer. Knots must be treated with knotting to prevent them showing, and all holes and cracks must be stopped before priming – there is a long standing argument between those who knot, stop and prime, and those who knot, prime and stop, but as long as the work is done properly the sequence is not critical. For timber exposed to severe conditions white lead primer is the most effective, but being a lead-based paint it must only be used where there is no alternative, and in no case where children have access. Undercoats are heavily pigmented and are coloured to blend with the final top coat. The final coat is usually gloss paint though matt paints are available, and these paints are produced in a very wide range of colours. Dark colours such as deep blue, black, and dark brown are liable to crack on surfaces exposed to continual hot sun, as they absorb the heat and cause considerable expansion and contraction of the underlying timber. The normal specification is for one coat of primer, two undercoats, and one top coat. Varnishes are sometimes used externally for decorative hardwoods to preserve the colour and grain, but they have a short life compared with paint systems, particularly since it is no longer possible to specify the twelve coats of increasingly thin varnish traditionally applied to external hardwoods which were expected to last for a generation. Paint manufacturers have their own individual formulae for paint which they are unwilling to reveal, so that it is advisable to specify that the entire paint system should be obtained from one manufacturer; mixing paints from different sources can cause disasters ranging from discoloration to the failure of the entire paint system.

9.2   METAL TREATMENT

Stainless steel is not normally painted or treated in any way, as it has a permanent self-finish resistant to most types of corrosion, though it may be affected by chemical emissions and may become dull from dust or sand abrasion. Mild steel, from which most railings and gates are made, is usually either galvanized, powder-coated, plastic-coated, or primed and painted.

Galvanizing

Heavy-duty galvanizing is carried out by the hot-dip process, where the finished item is dipped in a bath of molten zinc and allowed to drip; this gives a thick coating which will withstand wear well, but the coating may not penetrate small crevices perfectly. The alternative process is electro-galvanizing where the zinc coating is thinner but more consistently applied. Both processes depend on thorough preparation of the items before galvanizing and subsequent careful handling to prevent damage before fixing on site. Galvanizing is a tough finish best suited to agricultural and country-park work, where appearance is less important than durability and low maintenance costs. Damage to galvanizing may be made good by using cold-applied zinc paint, but this is not so durable as the initial processes. Decorative paint may be applied to galvanized metalwork, but it must first be primed with calcium plumbate primer, though as this contains lead, it must not be used in public areas likely to be used by children who may ingest particles during play.

Powder and plastic coatings

For prefabricated metalwork, powder coatings which are fused onto the metal at the factory provide a very good-looking smooth finish in a wide range of bright colours, but their disadvantage is that any site damage is difficult to make good, and matching paint will have to be used. Many proprietary railings, bollards, and signposts are powder coated.

Plastic-coated metal, usually nylon coating, is mainly used for handrails and similar light metalwork where heavy use is not expected. They are warmer to the hand in cold weather and therefore offer greater safety than cold steel. As with powder coatings, any damage must be made good with paint.

Painting metalwork

All steelwork should be thoroughly cleaned down with wire brushes or steel wool and every particle of mill-scale, grease, or rust removed to leave a clean bright surface before painting. The traditional treatment for mild steel is priming with red oxide, zinc chromate, or red lead primer, followed by one or two undercoats and one or two top coats. Red lead or, indeed, any lead-based paints are only permitted where there is no danger of people ingesting particles of the paint, and they are also dangerous to the workforce, so these hazards really limit their use to bridge works, road works and high-level railings where the public do not remain for any length of time but where long-life protection is important. Lead-based paints are more durable and weather-resistant than non-lead paints but they are more toxic. Red oxide of lead is a good rust preventative, and zinc chromate provides durability, and the two are often specified as a primer for steelwork.

A tough and adhesive paint mainly used for water tanks, gutters, and external steelwork where appearance is not critical is bituminous black paint, which is not primed but applied in two or three coats, but once it has been applied other paints cannot be applied afterwards. Tractor enamel is another weather-resistant paint, available in machinery manufacturer's bright colours, which is applied in several coats without a primer. Although it is used mainly for agricultural machinery, it has a useful role in places where petrol and oil resistance is important, such as garage forecourts and railings to parking areas.

Non-ferrous metals – that is, aluminium, brass, bronze, and copper – should be cleaned with fine wire wool or emery paper to remove oxide, grease and dirt and then either left natural or sealed with a clear epoxy resin coating. They may also be primed with zinc chromate before finishing with the same undercoats and finishing coats as described for steelwork.

10 SITE SUPERVISION OF FENCING WORK

The correct erection of fencing is not so critical as the construction of walls, but nevertheless, there are a number of points which should be watched on site. These include the following:

- Checking with a gauge that the size of line wires or wire mesh is as specified; 2.5 mm wire looks much the same as 3 mm wire but cannot take the same strain, nor is it as durable.
- Mesh fencing must be tied to the line wires at the specified intervals and with the specified tying wire: stainless steel, aluminium, or plastic coated wire. In good class work the top meshes are each clipped to the straining wire; this point should be checked.
- Where posts are driven into ground and not set in holes excavated with a mechanical post-holer, a crowbar or jumper bar should be driven dead vertical into the ground first to the full depth of the post to ensure that the post will go in vertically, as hitting a crooked post afterwards with a sledgehammer does little for its strength or stability and is unlikely to produce a permanently vertical post.
- Where timber is specified to be pressure-treated with preservative, it may be advisable to have a random sample post sawn through at its midpoint to check that the preservative treatment has penetrated the full depth of the timber and has not merely been applied to the surface.
- Precast concrete posts and precast post-and-panel fencing panels are liable to cracking if dropped or hit; they should be unloaded by hand or crane and stored on a clean dry level surface until wanted; they should never be dropped or thrown and they should be protected from oil and wood stainers. Cracking not only weakens the post but exposes the reinforcement to corrosion.

- Concrete for footings must be correctly and freshly mixed and must be poured within the proper setting time; the leftovers from the building contract will not do. Water for concrete must be of potable quality, and where fencing is erected some way away from the main site, clean water must be carried to the fencing site. The spoil from post holes should be removed from the site.
- Line wires should all be tensioned to the same degree, as one overtight wire takes too much strain.
- Nuts and bolts used for connecting fence and gate components must be properly washered (except for the heads of coach screws) to prevent them from being forced into the timber; it is much easier for the fence erector to omit a dropped washer than to search for it in long grass or mud.
- Where posts or stakes are specified as pointed they should be pointed before preservative treatment, not after, and timber cut on site must have the cut ends treated.
- Line wire, barbed wire, and barbed tape must be unreeled from the drum or coil and not lifted off in loops; this twists and strains the wire. Wire must be stored so that it cannot be flattened by other materials or by workmen walking on it, since this treatment causes irremovable kinks which create weak points liable to break under strain.
- If bolts are to be removed at a future date, they should be dipped in tallow before fixing. For example, gates may have to be removed from their posts (if lift-off hinges are not advisable) to allow the passage of extra-wide plant or machinery needed for ditch or pond dredging; kissing gates, which cannot be opened completely, are a type of gate where dismantling may be necessary from time to time. In this case it may be better to provide an additional lockable field gate for machinery access.
- Fences are not intended to provide support for the contractor's materials and equipment; they must be kept clear and protected if necessary till the end of the contract.
- Ensure that gates operate correctly and that there is sufficient tolerance on the fastenings to allow for movement and settlement. For example, self-closing gates should close quickly and smoothly without banging, and gate catches should hold the gate securely when it swings open and release it easily when operated.
- All notices and signs required by the client should be specified in the contract documents and fixed as part of the contract, not attached to any convenient point by a post-contract handyman.
- Posts must be driven using a proper manual or mechanical post-driver; the head of the post itself must not be hammered unless it is capped with a purpose-made sheet steel-cap. Check that the contractor is forming guide holes for the posts before driving them. The backfill of excavated material where post-holers are used should be well rammed back into the hole.

- Although service runs should have been surveyed and marked on the ground, this precaution is sometimes forgotten where fences are constructed, and the location of runs should be ascertained before deep post holes are made, since many services are only 450 mm below ground level, and it may be that the ground level has changed in the course of the contract. Particularly at risk are surface-water and land-drain runs, water supply pipes for swimming pools, ornamental pools, and irrigation systems, and electric cables for outdoor lighting.
- The tenons of rails in morticed fences should never be driven tightly into the mortice as the wood may swell and split the post.

BRITISH STANDARDS RELEVANT TO LAND-SCAPE CONSTRUCTION (WALLS, FENCES AND RAILINGS)

British Standards are continually being updated and revised. The reader should check that the latest standard is consulted when preparing constructional details and specifications.

STANDARD	SHORT TITLE
BS PD 6472: 1974	Guide to specifying the quality of building mortars
BS 12: 1989	Portland Cement
BS 187: 1978	Calcium silicate (flint/lime and sand/lime) bricks
BS 743: 1970	Materials for damp-proof courses
BS 882: 1983	Aggregates from natural sources for concrete
BS 890: 1972	Building limes
BS 1192: Pt 4: 1984	Recommendations for landscape drawings.

BS 1199: 1976 & AMD	Building sands from natural sources BS 1199: External rendering and floor screeds
BS 1200: 1976	Building sands from natural sources BS 1200: Sands for mortar for brickwork
BS 1217: 1986	Cast stone
BS 1377: Pt 1: 1990	Methods of tests for soils for civil engineering purposes. General requirements, sample preparation
BS 1377: Pt 2: 1990	Methods of tests for soils for civil engineering purposes. Classification requirements
BS 1377: Pt 4: 1990	Methods of tests for soils for civil engineering purposes. Compaction related tests
BS 1377: Pt 5: 1990	Methods of tests for soils for civil engineering purposes. Compressibility, permeability, and durability tests
BS 1377: Pt 9: 1990	Methods of tests for soils for civil engineering purposes. In situ tests
BS 1485: 1983 (1989)	Zinc coated hexagonal steel wire netting
BS 1722: Pt 4: 1986	Cleft chestnut pale fences
BS 1722: Pt 1: 1986	Chain link fences and gates and gate posts for fences up to 1.8m high
BS 1722: Pt 3: 1986	Strained wire fences
BS 1722: Pt 2: 1989	Rectangular wire mesh and hexagonal wire netting fences
BS 1722: Pt 10: 1990	Anti-intruder chain link fences
BS 1722: Pt 9: 1979	Mild steel fences with round or square verticals and flat standards and horizontals
BS 1722: Pt 6: 1976	Wooden palisade fences
BS 1722: Pt 7: 1986	Wooden post and rail fences
BS 1722: Pt 13: 1978	Chain link fences for tennis court surrounds
BS 1722: Pt 8: 1978	Mild steel (low carbon steel) continuous bar fences
BS 1722: Pt 12: 1990	Steel palisade fences
BS 1772: Pt 5: 1986	Close-boarded fences of oak and other timber from 1.05 m to 1.8 m high
BS 1881: Pts 1–209	Methods of testing concrete on site and in the laboratory
BS 2523: 1966 (1983)	Lead-based priming paints

190

BS 3049: 1976	Pedestrian guard rails
BS 3470: 1975	Field gates and posts in timber and steel
BS 3921: 1985	Clay bricks and blocks
BS 4008: 1973	Cattle grids on private roads
BS 4027: 1980	Sulphate resisting Portland cement
BS 4072: Pt 1: 1987	Wood preservation by means of copper/chromium, arsenic compositions: preservatives
BS 4072: Pt 2: 1987	Wood preservation by means of copper/chromium, arsenic compositions: two procedures of treatment.
BS 4102: 1990	Steel wire and wire products for fences
BS 4449: 1988	Carbon steel bars for the reinforcement of concrete
BS 4483: 1985	Steel fabric for the reinforcement of concrete
BS 4652: 1971 (1979)	Metallic zinc-rich priming paint (organic media)
BS 4721: 1981 (1986)	Ready mixed building mortars
BS 4729: 1990	Shapes and dimensions of special bricks
BS 4756: 1971 (1983)	Ready-mixed aluminium priming paints for woodwork
BS 4848: Pt 4: 1972 (1986)	Equal and unequal angles
BS 4887: Pt 1: 1986	Mortar admixtures. Air-entraining (plasticizing) admixtures
BS 4887: Pt 2: 1987	Mortar admixtures. Set retarding admixtures
BS 5075: Pt 1: 1982	Concrete admixtures: accelerating, retarding, and water reducing
BS 5075: Pt 2: 1982	Concrete admixtures: air-entraining admixtures
BS 5082: 1986	Water-borne priming paints for woodwork, for brush or spray application: paints with lead content below statutory labelling requirements
BS 5224: 1976	Masonry cement
BS 5262: 1976	Code of Practice for external rendered finishes
BS 5328: Pts 1–4: 1990	Guide to specifying concrete
BS 5358: 1986	Solvent-borne priming paints for woodwork for brush or spray application: paints with lead content below statutory labelling requirements

BS 5385: Pt 2: 1978	Code of Practice for external wall tiling and mosaics
BS 5390: 1976 (1984)	Code of Practice for stone masonry
BS 5450: 1977	Sizes of hardwoods and methods of measurements
BS 5589: 1989	Code of Practice for timber preservation
BS 5628: Pt 3: 1985	Code of Practice for the use of masonry, materials and components, design and workmanship
BS 5628: Pt 1: 1978 (1985)	Code of Practice for the use of unreinforced masonry, materials and components, design and workmanship
BS 5642: Pt 2: 1983	Copings of precast concrete, cast stone, clayware, slate and natural stone
BS 5707: Pt 1: 1979	Wood preservatives in organic solvents; general purpose applications including timber to be painted
BS 5709: 1979	Stiles, bridle gates and kissing gates
BS 5837: 1980	Code of Practice for trees in relation to construction
BS 5977: Pt 2: 1983	Concrete lintels
BS 6073: Pt 1: 1981	Precast concrete masonry units
BS 6100: Section 5.3: 1984	Bricks and blocks
BS 6180: 1982	Code of Practice for protective barriers in and about buildings, includes vehicle barriers up to 10 mph
BS 6571: Pt 4: 1989	Barrier type parking control
BS 6579: Pt 1: 1988	Safety fences and barriers for highways, components for tensioned corrugated beam safety fences on Z posts
BS 6649: 1985	Clay and calcium silicate modular bricks
BS 8000: Pt 3: 1989	Code of Practice for masonry (brick and block)
BS 8000: Pt 10: 1989	Code of Practice for plastering and rendering
BS 8110: 1985	Structural use of concrete
BS 8110: Pts 1,2,3: 1985	Structural use of concrete

GLOSSARY OF TERMS USED IN LANDSCAPE CONSTRUCTION (WALLS, FENCES AND RAILINGS

Additives	Chemicals added to mortar or concrete to enhance various properties; easy working, retarding, accelerating, rapid-hardening, colouring
Aggregate	Hard clean stone or natural gravel and stones, used for concrete
Angle irons	Rolled mild steel angle section posts
Ashlar	Finely finished accurately squared stone
Attached pier	Extra thickness of brickwork at the end or middle of a long freestanding wall which stabilises the structure and is often used to strengthen the wall where it carries a gate
Axed arch	Arch built of bricks cut to shape on site
Backing	The rear face of a wall where cheaper bricks are used on the unseen face
Ball stop	Fencing used round ball game areas
Bar railing	Railings formed of vertical steel or iron bars fixed to horizontal rails

Barbed tape	Steel wire with very sharp blades set along it
Bat	Specially cut part of a brick used to make up difficult bonds, also the leftover or broken bricks, hence the term 'throwing brickbats' since a whole brick is rather large for throwing
Bed	Brick bed: the surface on which the brick is laid Stone bed: the plane in which the stone lay before quarrying
Bed joint	The bed of mortar on which the brick is laid, or the vertical joint between voussoirs in an arch
Birdsmouth	A brick with a vee cut out of one end used for decorative work *or* a compression timber joint where one timber is cut at a double angle to fit into a corner between two other timber members, used for braces in gates
Bond	The chosen arrangement of bricks in the wall designed to give strength, stability, cohesion, and a good appearance
Brickie	The bricklayer
Bridle gate	Single gate designed to be opened and shut by horsemen
Bullnose	A brick with one corner rounded. A double bullnose has two adjoining corners rounded. Specials are made to fit external and internal angles. Bullnose bricks 'on the flat' are made for use as copings
Buttress	An attached pier, thicker at the bottom than at the top, built straight or at a sloping angle to support a wall which cannot take the design loads on its own. Not much used in brickwork today, but it can be a very attractive solution to the problem of strengthening a weak wall and is useful as a deterrent to prevent traffic from passing too close to the wall
Cant	Left or right handed. Brick with one corner cut off: similar to king closer but with a choice of angles. Specials are made to fit internal and external angles
Cast iron	Molten iron cast in a mould and not forged. Used where rust resistant heavy bollards or railing components are required. Very strong but brittle and can fracture or spall if hit
Cattle grid	Panel of steel bars which allows vehicles but not animals to pass along a road
Chain link	Interlocking wire fencing giving the appearance of chain-mail

Cleft	Timber not sawn but split along the natural grain of the wood
Close boarded	Fence of overlapping tapered boards fixed to horizontal rails
Closers	Small bats used to 'close' or make up the correct bond
Coffering	Recessed panels in brick or stone walls
Co-ordinating size	Brick and one joint
Coping	The capping laid on a wall to throw rain off the brickwork and to provide a hard frost and damage resistant finish
Corbel	Projecting course of brick used to support overhanging features
Course	One horizontal layer of bricks plus one mortar joint
Cownose	A brick with one rounded end
Crown	The top of an arch
Dogleg	Left or right handed. An oversize bent brick used for forming angles in walls
Double cant	A brick with two end corners cut off used for brick on edge copings. Specials are made to fit external and internal angles
DPC	A layer of impervious bricks, slates or other waterproof material laid between two courses of bricks to prevent damp creeping up or down the wall
Dry stone	Walls laid without mortar, used mostly for field walls
Efflorescence	Deposit of white salts on the face of brickwork caused by alternate wetting and drying cycles
Elliptical arch	Arch based on an ellipse
Extrados	The outside radius of an arch
Fair face	The face of the wall is carefully laid with all the bricks in the same plane, and usually requires the joints to be pointed after laying. A wall that is specified to be 'fair-faced' both sides must be at least 215 mm thick, as a half brick wall cannot be laid fair-face due to the variation in the bricks
Field fence	Fence of rectangular wire mesh to contain stock
Field gate	Plain timber or steel gate used to contain stock
Four centred	Arch based on linked curves drawn from four centres
Frog	The recess in the bed of a brick which provides a good key for mortar and reduces weight
Furniture	The hinges and fastenings of gates
Galvanizing	Coating steel with zinc by electro-plating or hot-dipping

Gauged arch	Arch built of bricks ground down to shape
Guard rails	Special railings designed to protect pedestrians from vehicles
Ha-Ha	Ditch with a fence in the bottom which does not obstruct views
Half bat	*or* Snapped header. A half brick used to make up bonds
Half round arch	Arch based on a semi-circle
Hanging post	*or* Swinging post, takes the weight of the gate and carries the hinges
Harling	Rendering with gravel incorporated giving a rough texture
Head joint	The joint between rings of bricks in a two, or more, ring arch
Herring-bone	Bricks set at 45 or 60 degrees, usually in panels
Hit-and-miss	Fence with gaps between boards on alternate sides
Hunting gate	Two-leaved gate designed to be opened and shut by horsemen
Intrados	The inside radius of an arch
Kiln dried	Timber dried in artificial heat
King closer	Right or left handed. A brick with one corner cut off
Kissing gate	Gate which allows pedestrians to pass but not stock or vehicles
Lacing course	One or more courses of ornamental brickwork
Masonry cement	Special cement: sand mixture with an air-entraining agent
Metric bricks	Bricks made in modular metric dimensions
Mortice	A socket cut in stone or timber to receive another timber or steel member, or a lock or bolt
OPSRC	Ordinary Portland Sulphate Resisting Cement used where sulphate conditions are present in the soil
Pales	Slender timbers wired closely together for temporary fencing
Palisades	Tall pointed steel or timber vertical bars set close together
Pallets	Timber platform on which bulk building supplies are delivered
Pebble-dash	Rendering with gravel thrown onto the wet surface
Perforated	Bricks with holes through the bed face
Perpend	The vertical joint between two bricks. The perpends in a wall should be seen as true vertical lines
Pickets	Small pointed timbers set close together in open fencing
Pier	Strictly speaking a freestanding column of brick-

	work, usually supporting a beam
Pilaster	A shallow projecting pier on the face of a wall, usually intended as a decorative feature
Plinth	A thicker section of brick or stone at the base of a wall to strengthen it and to protect it against vehicles
Plinth brick	A brick with a bevelled top edge used to construct plinths. The purpose of the bevel is to avoid the water which would lie on the projecting surface of a standard brick
Pointing	The process of going over mortar joints previously left recessed while the bricks were being laid and finishing them with special mortar or special tools to give a profile to the joint
Pole-barrier	A pole which is lifted to allow vehicles to enter an area
Post	Vertical timber, steel or concrete member supporting a gate or fence
Post and rail	Timber fences with horizontal rails nailed or mortised to posts
Post and wire	Fence constructed of posts with lines of wire
Quarry sap	Moisture present in freshly quarried stone
Queen closer	A half brick cut lengthways, used to make up a quarter brick bond in alternate courses
Quoin	A corner of a brick or stone wall
Racking	Staggering the courses at the end of part of a wall so that later brickwork will bond well into it
Radial brick	Headers, stretchers and bricks on edge made with a range of radii used for small radius arches and curved work where the radius is too small to allow standard bricks to be used
Rail	Horizontal member of a timber or metal fence
Ready mix	A cement:lime:sand, cement:sand, or sand:lime mixture supplied ready mixed to the correct proportions. Water is added on site
Relieving arch	Arch which supports part of the weight of the wall
Ridge tiles	Special shaped tiles laid along the ridge of a tiled roof
Rise	The height of an arch from the springing to the crown
Rough arch	Arch built of standard bricks
RSJ	British Standard Rolled Steel Joist
Rubble	Natural stone more or less squared before laying
Segmental arch	Arch based on a segment of a circle
Specials	Bricks of non-standard shape used for angles, arches and curves

197

Spur stone	Short strong stone or concrete post used to protect openings
Squint	Left or right hand. A brick with one end cut at two angles for forming angles in walls
Stanchion	Vertical post forming part of a rail and stanchion railing
Stile	Hanging stile is the vertical member of a gate which takes the hinges; swinging, closing, or shutting stile is the vertical member which takes the latch or bolt
Stilted arch	An arch with a short straight vertical section at the springing
String course	Single course of projecting ornamental brickwork
Swing post	*or* slamming, clapping, or shutting post takes the thrust of the closing gate
Tenon	The shaped end of a rail which fits into the mortice
Tile creasing	Two courses of tiles laid lapped, as a DPC below the coping
Trip rail	Low rail used to protect grassed areas against vehicles
UB	British Standard Universal Beam
Voussoirs	The standard or special radius bricks used to form an arch. Firms such as Taperall Taylor will cut bricks to any arch profile required
Wall ties	Wire or metal strips used to tie two skins of brickwork together
Weathered	With the top edge sloped downwards to throw off rainwater
Wind tunnel	The funnelling of wind between high buildings, increasing its force
Work size	Actual size of brick
Wrought iron	Iron which has been forged hot. Used for ornamental railings and gates; tough and rust resistant

BIBLIOGRAPHY OF BOOKS RELEVANT TO LANDSCAPE CONSTRUCTION (WALLS, FENCES AND RAILINGS)

Ashurst, J. and N. (1988), *Practical Building Conservation Vols 1, 2, 3*, Aldershot, Gower.

Beazley, E., (1960), *Design and Detail of the Space between Buildings* 1st ed London, Architectural Press

Brick Development Association
    various publications

Cement and Concrete Association (now called British Cement Association)
    various publications

Cutler, D.F., and Richardson, I.D.K., (1989) *Tree Roots and Buildings*, 2nd ed., London Construction Press

Jaggard, W.R., and Drury, F.E. (1947), *Architectural Building Construction Vols I and II*, Cambridge, Cambridge University Press

Korff, J.O.A. (1983), *The Design of Freestanding Walls*, Brick Development Association

McKay, W. and J. (1971), *Building Construction Vol I*, 5th ed, London, Longman

Mitchell's Building Series (1983) *Structures and Fabric Part I*

Nash, W.G., *Brickwork vol, I, II and III*, S. Thornes

Spon's Landscape Handbook (1986), ed. Derek Lovejoy Partnership 3rd ed, London, Spon

INDEX